AF425568

Debarim Publishing
21566 Main St, Howe, OK 74940
www.debarimpublishing.com

Paperback ISBN-13: 979-8-9932402-3-7
Ebook ISBN-13: 979-8-9932402-4-4

This book is lovingly dedicated to Nava, my bride and best friend whose sacrificial love and devotion has taught me more about the love of Messiah than words can adequately express.

The Trinity
Controversy
& The Hidden
Codes of Divinity

TABLE OF CONTENTS

Part 1

The Trinity Controversy

Introduction

"The internet has provided an open pulpit for anyone who wants to be a Bible teacher. The advantage is that anyone can teach the Bible online and influence hundreds, or perhaps thousands, of people. The disadvantage of this is that anyone can teach the Bible online and influence hundreds or perhaps thousands of people." [Dr. Daniel Botkin in Gates of Eden Vol. 30 No. 5, page 11]

"BUT, PAGAN RELIGIONS ALL HAVE TRINITIES THAT PRE-DATE THE BIBLE!"

The following are excerpts from an article entitled How Ancient Trinitarian Gods Influenced Adoption of the Trinity Posted on Jul 22, 2011, by United Church of God.

Marie Sinclair, Countess of Caithness, in her 1876 book Old Truths in a New Light, states: "It is generally, although erroneously, supposed that the doctrine of the Trinity is of Christian origin. Nearly every nation of antiquity possessed a similar doctrine. [The early Catholic theologian] St. Jerome testifies unequivocally, 'All the ancient nations believed in the Trinity'" (p. 382).

James Bonwick summarized the story well on page 396 of his 1878 work, Egyptian Belief and Modern Thought: "It is an undoubted fact that more or less all over the world the deities are in triads. This rule applies to eastern and western hemispheres, to north and south.

"Further, it is observed that, in some mystical way, the triad of three persons is one. The first is as the second or third, the second as first or third, the third as first or second; in fact, they are each other, the same individual being. The definition of Athanasius, who lived in Egypt, applies to the trinities of all heathen religions."

Few understand how the Trinity doctrine came to be accepted - several centuries after the Bible was completed! Yet its roots go back much farther in history.

"The origin of the conception is entirely pagan."

-End of Excerpts-

This information is enough to convince many to search no further. If it originated with pagans, why even consider it to be a biblical truth? But here are two questions that need to be addressed:

Question 1: What spirit is it that inspires pagan beliefs?

Answer: Lucifer

Question 2: When does Lucifer ever have an original thought?

Answer: Never

Our Adversary is an imitator. He only mimics what he has seen and what he knows about God.

THROWING THE PROVERBIAL BABY OUT WITH THE BATH WATER

Years ago, I met a Jewish family who had converted to Catholicism. My feelings were mixed. I thought it was wonderful that a Jewish family had come to a saving knowledge that "Jesus" came to die in their place, to take away their sins, and they now called Him their "Lord and Savior." But these were not Messianic Jews. They were Catholics through and through. They went to church on Sunday, prayed to Mary, ate pork and shellfish, and celebrated Christmas and Easter. What had they done? They reasoned that if Judaism had not told them the truth about "Jesus," they must not have told them the truth about Torah being "abolished." They threw the proverbial baby out with the bathwater.

The same is true for many Christians who have come to a "Hebraic/Torah Awakening" that is so prevalent in our modern times. When they begin to learn that the Biblical Sabbath and Feast Days were not abolished, and that God was not doing away with the dietary laws when Peter got his vision, etc., they start to wonder what else the Christian world may have gotten wrong. Perhaps they were not told the truth about the nature of God and even the deity of Y'shua. Without sufficient knowledge of the Scriptures, these are open prey to online "teachers" who only tell part of the story. Unfortunately, such a vacuum leaves them open to receive whatever is contrary to what they were told before, whether good or bad, true or false.

"THEY BELIEVE THAT, SO I BELIEVE THIS"

Forming a theological viewpoint based on a reaction to someone else's theological viewpoint is simply not logical. We must examine ourselves [2 Corinthians 13:5] and lose all false presuppositions. Our beliefs must be solely based upon the truth of the Word of God [John 17:17], and that is not an unachievable task.

"BUT THE TERM 'TRINITY' IS NOT FOUND IN THE BIBLE"

It was the early Church father, Tertullian [155-220 A.D.], who coined the term "trinity" to describe the multiplicity of the Oneness of God, apparent throughout the Scriptures. Mystic Judaism calls this mysterious unity "Sephirot," another term not found in the Bible. Israeli believers in Y'shua today use the term "Echdut Elohim," meaning "the Unity of God." Benjamin Sommer, in his book, Bodies of God, calls it "Fluidity." None of these terms can be found in the Bible. However, whatever you choose to call it, as long as you are affirming that the Father, the Son, and the Set-apart Spirit are fully God, and there is only one God, you are in line with the texts of what the Hebrew Scriptures reveal about the nature of God.

TRINITY IS BIBLICAL

God is transcendent, existing outside of time and space. This is why we are told in the Gospel of John;

*No one has ever seen God; but **the one and only God, [monogenais Theos]** in the Father's embrace, has made Him known. [John 1:18 TLV with Greek transliteration inserted]*

And in Exodus 33, we read;

...you cannot see My face, for no man can see Me and live.
[Exodus 33:20 TLV]

Nevertheless, we read where God has "appeared" or "revealed" Himself in a small-scale manifestation, in time and space, to interact with man.

*And **יהוה** **appeared** to him by the Terbinth trees of Mamre while he was sitting in the tent door in the heat of the day. So he lifted his eyes and looked and saw **three men** standing opposite him...*
[Genesis 18:1-2a ISR version]

[For more on this passage, see Chapter 6 - EMENDATIONS OF THE SOPHERIM and Chapter 7 - THE 3 YHWH'S]

My first question for anti-trinitarians is, "Have you read the entire Bible?" If so, I would say there is quite a bit you missed. Having been a student of the Scriptures for many years, I am amazed whenever I hear someone say they are a serious student of the Bible, yet they do not believe in the triune nature of God revealed in the Bible.

I am writing this book in two sections. The first part, entitled THE TRINITY CONTROVERSY, is meant to address the many issues related to this controversial topic directly from the face texts of Scripture. Section 2, entitled THE HIDDEN CODES OF DIVINITY, is an exploration into the Equidistant Letter Sequences that are embedded within the face text of Scripture. It will also include the mystery of gematria [the numerical value of Hebrew letters and phrases] and the divine significance of numbers.

All Scripture references for the Tanak/Old Testament are from the TLV [Tree of Life Version] and all for the Brit Chadashah/New Testament are from the AENT [Aramaic English New Testament] unless otherwise noted.

It is my hope and prayer that what I am presenting here will bring a clearer understanding of what the Scriptures contain and what they reveal about the mysterious and unfathomable nature of God. May you, the reader, experience His presence in the process of this study and be arrested by His incomprehensibility.

Creator of the Universe

The Bible tells us that Y'shua is the Creator of everything visible and invisible.

> *"...then I was the craftsman beside Him..."*
> *[Proverbs 8:30a]*

> *and by him was created everything that is in heaven and on earth, all that is visible and all that is invisible, whether thrones or dominions or principalities or powers; everything was through him and was created by him.*
> *[Colossians 1:16]*

> *But in these latter days, He has conversed with us by His Son, whom He has constituted heir of all things, and by whom He made the worlds;*
> *[Hebrews 1:2]*

> *Everything existed through His hands, and without Him, not even one thing existed of the things which have existed.*
> *[John 1:3]*

The following are two excerpts from a Rabbi Tzvi Nassi:

On opening my Bible, the very first sentence drew my mind forcibly into deep meditation. "In the beginning Elohim [He] created." I cannot make "He created," being in the singular, agree grammatically with "Elohim" in the plural. There must therefore be a logical agreement between the noun and the verb.

Elohim is compounded of two words, El, Hym, i.e. They God. The plural is expressed by the letter yod as in Ecclesiastes 12:1, "Remember now thy Creator." The letter yod in "Thy Creator" expresses the plural, and we should therefore translate "Thy Creators." He that is wise will understand it.

[The Great Mystery: How Can Three Be One? And Yeshua in the Ancient Hebrew, pg.13, by Rabbi Tzvi Nassi & Dr. Al Garza]

Sustainer of all Matter

The Bible tells us that Y'shua is the Sustainer of all in the material universe.

who is the splendor of His glory and the exact image of His nature, and upholds
all by the power of His Word;
[Hebrews 1:3a]

He existed before all things, and He holds everything together.
[Colossians 1:17 CJB-Complete Jewish Bible]

Scientists have determined that the atom defies the laws of physics and magnetism. Scientists cannot fully explain the mechanism that prevents the negatively charged electrons from collapsing into the positively charged protons within the atom. The answer is in the verse above. It is Y'shua who holds every atom in the universe together.

The First & the Last; The Beginning & the End

In the book of Revelation, John writes that when Y'shua appeared to him to give him this revelation, Y'shua referred to Himself as the "first and the last, the beginning and the end." This phrase shows up seven times in the Bible. Four of them are quotes from Y'shua in Revelation 1:8 & 17, 21:6 & 22:13. The other three are found in the Tanak in Isaiah 41:4, 44:6 and 48:12. Clearly, this is divine speech since it is יהוה YHWH who is speaking in the book of Isaiah. Unarguably, it would be blasphemy for anyone other than יהוה YHWH to make such a lofty claim.

Hebrew, like Chinese, originated as a picture language. The pictographs of the Sacred Name that predate Paleo and Modern forms of the letters reveal a startling message.

Yod ['] = Hand
Hey [ה] = A man standing with his arms up to get your attention as if to say, "Look."
Vav [ו] = A Tent Peg or Nail
Hey [ה] = "Look"

"Look at the Hand. Look at the Nail."

Then I will pour out on the house of David and the inhabitants of Jerusalem a spirit of grace and supplication, when they look toward Me, whom they pierced.
[Zechariah 12:10]

The Alef & the Tav

"I am the Alpha and the Omega" is how this passage is translated in the Greek of Revelation 1:8, 21:6 & 22:13. Subsequently, most English versions render it this way. However, the Brit Chadashah/New Testament was originally written in Aramaic. In the Aramaic Peshitta, this phrase appears as "I am the Alef and the Tav." Alef [א] and Tav [ת] are the first and last letters of both the Aramaic and Hebrew alef-bets. The Alef and Tav appear throughout the Hebrew Tanak as a direct object marker in a sentence. It is not considered a translatable word; therefore, its placement throughout the Tanak is not reflected in the Greek translation of the Tanak, known as the Septuagint [circa 250BCE].

In the pictographs of the Hebrew letters, Alef is an ox head and represents ultimate strength, aka the strength of YHWH. Its numerical value is 1 and therefore also represents God Himself.

The pictograph form of Tav is a Cross. This 22nd letter of the alef-bet represents a "sign" and "covenant."

Genesis 22 gives us the account of the Akeidah [the binding of Isaac], which was a parabolic foreshadowing of the crucifixion taking place at the very location of the crucifixion two thousand years beforehand.

Psalm 22 gives us prophetic foreshadowing of the crucifixion, with verses such as "My God, My God, why have You forsaken me?" [v1]

and "they pierced my hands and my feet" [v17].

CROSS VS EXECUTION STAKE

Those who have been persuaded to believe it was NOT a Cross that Y'shua died upon are incapable of seeing the open secrets that are otherwise clear.

It is a common controversy that exists. Was Y'shua crucified on a Cross or an execution Stake? Sculptures and artworks portray men crucified by both methods. There is an obvious prejudice that causes many to lean towards an execution Stake rather than a Cross. After all, isn't the Cross derived from "Pagan religions"? Denial of facts based on a false presupposition is simply foolish. To insist that Y'shua had to be crucified on an execution Stake rather than a Cross because one believes the symbol is of Pagan origin [or for some other reason], is the same kind of reasoning anti-trinitarians use to deny the obvious evidence shown throughout the Scriptures to the contrary.

In the original Aramaic language of the New Testament, we find the following;

*And the disciples told him, "We have seen our Master!" But he said to them, "Unless I see **the places of the nails [דוכיתא דצצא** Duukyatha Tsetsey] in his hands and I place my fingers in them, and I stretch forth my hand in his side, I will not believe."*
[John 20:25]

Both the word for "places" [Duukyatha] and the word for "nails" [Tsetsey] are plural in the original language of Aramaic. It only takes a single nail [the size of a tent peg] to be driven through both wrists when a man is crucified on a Stake. It takes two nails to crucify him on a Cross.

Here is an example of an insight that can be missed or dismissed due to a false presupposition. The Hebrew word for "religion" is דת, Dat. It is formed from the letter Dalet [ד] and Tav [ת]. In the pictograph forms

of the letters, Dalet is a Door and Tav is a Cross. A person finds true
"religion" when they have entered through the Door that brings them
to the Cross!

Y'shua is the Strength [א] of the Covenant [ת]. It is only through His
sacrificial death on the Cross that we obtain a Covenant with God.

An amazing Equidistant Letter Sequence [ELS] was discovered in
Psalm 22, which I share in Chapter 34.

Plural Verbiage in the Hebrew Text

In Genesis 20:13, Abraham is talking to King Abimelech about the God who "caused me to wander..." The form of the verb "caused" is third person plural. Rather than "Ta'ah" [third person singular], we find התעו Hitoo [third person plural]. This literally translates to "**THEY** caused." This third-person plural form of a verb also occurs in Genesis 35:7. This portion of Scripture tells us of the time when Jacob went to BethEl to build an altar to the God who appeared to him. The third-person singular of "appeared" is "Nigla"; however, the verb form for "appeared" is third-person plural, "נגלו" (Nigloo). This means that the literal translation should be rendered "**THEY** appeared...".

Emendations of the Sopherim

In the fourth century BC or earlier, those scribes whose responsibility it was to preserve the Hebrew Texts of Scripture took it upon themselves to make changes to the original texts, to edit out passages that posed a disturbing challenge to their understanding of God's existence. Thankfully, "the Sopherim," as they are known, kept meticulous records and left evidence of what they had done, making notations in the margins of the texts, called the "Massorah." One can read about this from the Companion Bible, Appendix 32, or the explanatory notes of THE SCRIPTURES [ISR Version] published by the INSTITUTE FOR SCRIPTURE RESEARCH.

Under the pretense that the name of God was too sacred to speak, they replaced the tetragrammaton [the Sacred Name of YHWH] with "Adonai" or some other circumlocution in 134 places of Scripture. However, they left the Sacred Name unchanged in another 6,823 places. So what was the actual reason they only made 134 emendations? The Sopherim were uncomfortable with what they read, not the name itself. They changed it only in the places that disturbed their religious sensitivities. One of those places was anytime that YHWH seemed to be in multiple places simultaneously. The emendations are numbered in the margin of the Massorah. Emendations #1,#2 & #3 are found in Genesis 18, where we read of the first visible appearance of God to man. Verse 1 states that "YHWH appeared" and He appeared as "three men" [v2]. Moses wrote that Abraham addressed these three men as "YHWH" [v3]. Then we find emendations #4 & #5 in Genesis 19, where we read of the "two messengers" who went to Sodom. In verse 18, Moses writes that Lot addressed these two messengers as "YHWH."

The 3 YHWHs

How can they [the Three] be One?
Are they verily One, because we call them One?
How the Three can be one, can only be known through the revelation of the
Holy Spirit.
[Zohar II 43b]

The appearance of the three visitors in Genesis 18 & the two in Genesis 19 is foundational to this topic of the Trinity. Dr. Al Garza has done an excellent job covering this issue in his book The Great Mystery: How Can Three Be One? The following are excerpts from that book:

"and YHWH appeared..." [Genesis 18:1]

The Hebrew word for "appeared" means to literally be seen and to present oneself. This means that YHWH visibly appeared to Abraham, but what did Abraham see?

"And he [Abraham] lift up his eyes, and looked, and, lo, three men stood by him: and when he saw [them], he ran to meet them from the tent door, and bowed himself toward the ground," [Genesis 18:2]

We read that Abraham lifted up his eyes to see three men standing by him, ran to meet THEM, and prostrated himself to the ground as an act of worship. Is this how you greet two Angels with YHWH?

Abraham greeted them all the same, and the next verse is astonishing.

"And said, 'YHWH, if now I have found favor [grace in Hebrew] in thy sight, pass not away, I pray thee, from thy servant:' " [Genesis 18:3]

Your English translation will not include the name of God but will likely say "my Lord or Lords." This is not the correct translation for this verse. The Hebrew is Adonai with the Hebrew qamets vowel, which is ONLY used for YHWH and only YHWH. The Bible translates this verse correctly, using the name YHWH in the passage. Many Jewish commentaries on this verse try to explain it by saying that Abraham was addressing YHWH, not the two messengers, but, as we will see, that is not the case.

I need to explain that when the Masoretes were writing the Hebrew Bible, they changed the word YHWH to Adonai with the vowel qamets, so that when you read Adonai with qamets, you were reading a place in the passage with the name of God, namely YHWH. This was noted in their margins for preferred reading. Dr. Ginsberg has collected these changes in his book, Introduction to the Messorecto-Critical Edition of the Hebrew Bible (Ktav Publishing House, Inc.). New York. So, in Genesis 18:3, you should be reading YHWH, not "my Lord or Lords." Let us now continue.

"And THEY said," [Genesis 18:5]

In verse 5, we read "they said," but who is the **THEY**? It appears that all three are speaking in one voice. This type of conversation occurs in the Bible only when God, or YHWH, speaks. In Exodus, Moses heard VOICES plural from the mountain. We see this again in verse 9, after Abraham brought THEM food and stood by THEM as they ate.

"And THEY said unto him, Where [is] Sarah thy wife? And he said, Behold, in the tent." [Genesis 18:9]

Here they speak again in one voice and ask for Sarah, his wife. How can Angels speak in one voice with YHWH? This is unheard of in the Hebrew Bible. No such thing happens. Only YHWH speaks this way in a plural voice. In verse 10, we read that YHWH speaks in the singular as well.

"And HE said," *[Genesis 18:10]*

YHWH then asks why his wife Sarah laughed when He told him that He would return when he had his son. We now know that YHWH is really present with them, but again, the question is: how many YHWHs are there? So far, we see that all three speak as one voice, and at least one of them is actually YHWH, who speaks. Let us now continue.

"And YHWH said, Shall I hide from Abraham that thing which I do;"
[Genesis 18:17]

Here we read YHWH asking a question to the other two messengers, but it is only YHWH who answers himself in verse 20. YHWH then says HE will go down to Sodom and Gomorrah in verse 21.

"I will go down now [YHWH speaking], and see whether they have done altogether according to the cry of it, which is come unto me; and if not, I will know." *[Genesis 18:21]*

Here, YHWH says to the messengers that HE will go down, but in verse 22, the two men went toward Sodom, and YHWH stood with Abraham. Why did YHWH say he was going but didn't? Let us continue reading.

"And YHWH went his way, as soon as he had left communing with Abraham: and Abraham returned unto his place." *[Genesis 18:33]*

After Abraham finished pleading and negotiating with YHWH about how many righteous people could be in Sodom, YHWH went away. The only ones left were Abraham and the two messengers who left for Sodom. When the two messengers arrived at Sodom, Lot did something unusual.

"And there came two messengers to Sodom at evening; and Lot sat in the gate of Sodom: and Lot seeing [them] rose up to meet them; and he bowed himself with his face toward the ground;" [Genesis 19:1]

Lot went to meet them, and when he did, he did what Abraham did. Lot bowed himself with his face to the ground, and the two messengers let him. The messengers never told him to rise because they were only Angels. They expected the worship to be as before with Abraham. Lot then asked them to stay, as did Abraham. The two messengers then spoke as one again in verse 2.

"And THEY said, No; but we will abide in the open square all night."
[Genesis 19:2]

It isn't until verse 13 and following that things become interesting and clear to the reader of who these two men and messengers are.

"For we will destroy this place, because the cry of them is grown great before the face of YHWH; and YHWH hath sent us to destroy it." [Genesis 19:13]

In this verse, the two messengers explain that they were sent to destroy the city by YHWH because the sins of Sodom are great before the face of YHWH. Does this verse prove that the two messengers are just messengers and not YHWH? Let us continue.

"And it came to pass, when they had brought them outside, that he said, Escape for thy life; look not behind, neither stay anywhere in the plain; escape to the mountain, lest thou be consumed." [Genesis 19:17]

When the two messengers took them outside the city and told Lot and his family to flee, Lot answered them and addressed them by the name YHWH and said, if he were THEIR servant and if he found grace in THEIR eyes, then they would spare him and his family in order to make it to the mountain.

"And Lot said TO THEM, Oh no, YHWH: Behold now, thy servant hath found grace in thy sight, and thou hast magnified thy mercy, which thou hast showed

unto me in saving my life; and I cannot escape to the mountain, lest some evil take me, and I die:" [Genesis 19:18-19]

Lot addressed them as YHWH, according to this verse and according to Dr. C.D. Ginsberg. This was one of the verses that was changed from YHWH to Adonai with qamets. Out of the 142 places, this was one of them, along with Genesis 18:3. There should be no doubt about this change, since it was discovered in the margins of the MT Hebrew manuscripts. The two messengers reply, telling Lot that he has found grace in their eyes and that they cannot destroy the city until they arrive safely in the city called Zoar. There is NO place in the entire Hebrew Bible where mere Angels or created beings can give grace like they did unless they are YHWH. This grace passage is the same one that was spoken by Abraham to YHWH, and now the messengers respond with grace to Lot. Either these men are YHWH, or the name YHWH has no special meaning, and anyone can take the name and apply it to themselves in the Bible. The very next verse tells you who these men are.

"And YHWH rained upon Sodom and upon Gomorrah brimstone and fire from YHWH out of heaven;" [Genesis 19:24]

There should be little doubt that these two messengers and men were YHWH who rained down fire and brimstone from YHWH in heaven since YHWH left Abraham and went back to heaven. ALL of the evidence for three men who were ALL called YHWH is overwhelming. The Hebrew Bible and the Jewish Hebrew scholar Dr. Ginsberg makes note of the changes in the MT, which puts these men to be more than just Angels or mere messengers, as many suggest.

The word used in the English Bibles for these men is " angels," which is a Greek term and not a Hebrew word. The word "Malak," literally in Hebrew, means "Messenger," not "Angel." The term Malak and even Angel can be used of anyone, including YHWH himself, in Genesis 16 by Hagar and in Genesis 22, where the Messenger of YHWH is the one who blesses Abraham and takes credit for everything Abraham is about to do and accomplish in obeying his voice.....They were YHWH, ONE, and revealed themselves as men and messengers.

When we look at the Hebrew name YHWH, it literally means "He Exists," but in Hebrew words can be divided to represent a deeper meaning... Each of those letters by itself can represent the name of God, YHWH.

Y=YHWH
H=YHWH
W= "and " in Hebrew
H=YHWH

The three letters ALL represent YHWH in Hebrew, with the Waw meaning "and". Only individuals who are deeply immersed in ancient Hebrew will confirm what I just stated. [end of excerpts from The Great Mystery: How Can Three Be One? And Yeshua in the Ancient Hebrew by Rabbi Tzvi Nassi & Dr. Al Garza ThD, PhD, pages 121 -130]

"Eliezer's father said to him: Come and see the mystery of the word Y'H'W'H: there are three steps, each existing by itself; nevertheless, they are One, and so united that one cannot be separated from the other."
[Zohar, vol iii, p.65, Amsterdam Edition]

Son of Man

"Also, He has given him authority to execute judgment, because He is the Son of Man." [John 5:27 CJB]

In this passage, Y'shua states that He has been given authority, referencing Himself as the "Son of Man." Where do we see the first use of this terminology, and what are its implications? Its first use is found in Daniel 7:13-14. Daniel is explaining a vision where he describes a mysterious second figure with eternal power who is given dominion over all the tribes and nations of the earth. It is said here that He will have authority over all, and His dominion will be without end. This mention of a second figure with power, authority & eternal dominion links us to other similar prophetic passages:

Of the increase of His government and shalom, there will be no end...
[Isaiah 9:7]

Awake, O sword, against My shepherd, against the man who is My companion!
[Zech 13:7]

But you, Bethlehem Ephrathah - least among the clans of Judah- from you will come out to Me One to be ruler in Israel, One whose goings forth are from of old, from days of eternity.
[Micah 5:2]

The Mysterious Presence

The Torah reveals that God dwells in two sanctuaries simultaneously without ceasing to be One God. He dwells in His heavenly sanctuary [Deut 4:36 & 26:15] and with His people on earth [Ex 40:33-35 & Lev 26:11-12]. In Leviticus 26:12, we find the word התהלכתי "hetalachti" in the phrase "I will walk among you," which is listed as #3212 in the Strong's Concordance. In Genesis 3:8, we are told that God "walked" in the Garden of Eden. The Hebrew word in this passage is also listed as Strong's #3212 as it shares a common root. The Stone Edition of the Artscroll Chumash translates that word in Genesis 3:8 as "manifest." According to the verbiage, God actually lived among His people as He did with Adam in the Garden. One God dwells simultaneously among His people while dwelling in heaven, just as Y'shua told Nicodemus.

...the Son of Man is He who is in heaven [John 3:13b]

The Angel of the Name

When Moses stood before the burning bush, was it a Messenger/Angel he was speaking with or YHWH Himself? We are initially told that the "Messenger" appeared to Moses [v2], but in the remainder of the chapter, it is YHWH Himself who converses directly with Moses. The following is a quote from a non-messianic Jewish professor, Benjamin Sommer, from his book entitled Bodies of God;

The famous fire in this passage, which burned IN the bush without burning the bush, is nothing other than a small-scale manifestation of God. [Benjamin Sommer, Bodies of God, pp 41-42]

Speaking of Gideon's encounter with the "Angel of the Lord" in Judges 6:12-16, Sommer writes on page 43 of Bodies of God;

The text variously identifies the speaker as YHWH [vs 14-15] and YHWH's MALAKH [vs 12, 20 & 21]. Indeed, God's visitor sometimes speaks in the first person of God [vs 14 & 16] and sometimes in the third [v 12]. One might want to argue that YHWH was located in heaven and spoke through a lower-ranking divine being sent to earth with a message, but it is specifically YHWH who turns His face toward Gideon in verse 14. At the same time, we are told [v 22] that Gideon saw YHWH's MALAKH who left the place [v 21].

The text seems self-contradictory only if one insists that the "Angel" is a being separate from YHWH. On the other hand, if one can understand this "Angel/Messenger" as a small-scale manifestation of God, aka God Himself as His own "Messenger," the text coheres perfectly well.

Concerning YHWH's MALAKH, this is what we read in Exodus;

Behold, I send an Angel before thee, to keep thee in the way, and to bring thee into the place which I have prepared. Beware of him, and obey His voice, provoke Him not; for He will not pardon your transgressions: for My Name is in Him.
[Exodus 23:20-21 KJV].

Pardoning transgressions is an attribute that belongs solely to God Himself. The Hebraic understanding of "Name" is "Authority." This Messenger shares the Name/Authority of YHWH. The people were told not to "provoke" this Messenger lest he not pardon their transgressions. Paul makes reference to this matter when He writes in his first epistle to the Corinthians;

Neither let us tempt the Mashiyach, as some of them tempted: and serpents destroyed them. [1 Corinthians 10:9]

In the following chapter, we will examine the Gospel account of the Messiah exercising this authority to forgive sins.

Forgiving Sins

Some people came bringing to Him a paralyzed man, carried by four men. When they couldn't get near Yeshua because of the crowd, they removed the roof where He was. After digging through, they lowered the mat on which the paralyzed man was lying. Yeshua, seeing their faith, said to the paralyzed man, "Son, your sins are forgiven." But some of the Torah scholars were sitting there, questioning in their hearts, "Why does this fellow speak like this? **He blasphemes! Who can pardon sins but God alone?"**
[Mark 2:3-7 TLV]

When Y'shua pardoned the sins of the paralytic, before healing him, we are told that the scribes accused him of blasphemy, saying, "Who is able to forgive sins except the one Elohim?" And it surely would have been blasphemy had He not had the authority to do so.

Y'shua remains throughout all time to be the One who keeps us in the way, to bring us into the place which God has prepared for us. We must obey His voice, or He will not pardon our transgressions.

"I and the Father are One."

Another occurrence of what would otherwise be considered blasphemy is found in the 10th chapter of the Gospel of John, where Y'shua declares that He and the Father are "One" [John 10:30]. The following verse states,

Once again, the Judeans picked up rocks in order to stone Him.
[John 10:31 CJB]

In fact, two verses later, the text tells us clearly the people's reason as to why they wanted to stone Him.

*The Judeans replied, "We are not stoning you for any good deed, but **for** **blasphemy** -because you, who are only a man, are **making yourself to be God.***
[John 10:33 CJB]

A claim to be One with the Father would certainly be blasphemy and a transgression worthy of a stoning if it were not true.

Messianic prophecy provides many indicators to recognize when the Messiah has arrived. Is a claim of equality with God the Father one of those identifiers? In other words, should we expect the true Messiah to make this claim when He arrives on the scene of humanity?

The prophet Zechariah tells us this;

"O Sword, awake against My Shepherd, against the man who is My companion,"
declares יהוה of Hosts.
[Zechariah 13:7 ISR Version]

The word translated "Companion" is עמית Amiyth. Strong's #5997. Various renderings of this word include Associate, Companion, Comrade, Kindred, Fellow, Neighbor.

According to what is revealed in this prophecy in the book of Zechariah, we can expect the Messiah to claim His companionship, comradeship, kindredness, etc., with God. In otherwords, if the Messiah does not claim co-equality with God, He is not the true Messiah!

THE STONE

The Stone the builders rejected has become the cornerstone.
[Psalm 118:22]

He who rejects the Son rejects the Father. This is revealed in the Hebrew word for "Stone." It is spelled with three letters.

אבן

The first two letters, Alef and Bet, spell AV, meaning FATHER. The middle and last letters spell the word BAYN, meaning SON.

The Son and the Father are indivisibly One!

I Am

In John's Gospel, Y'shua makes an astounding statement that was met with a near stoning from the people who heard it.

...Yes indeed! Before Avraham came into being, I AM
[John 8:58 CJB]

Most English Bibles will capitalize the "I AM" to reflect the gravity of His statement and the incident that ensued because of it. The Aramaic phrase that Y'shua spoke was אנא איתי Ena Ithay, which translates to "I WAS" in the AENT [Aramaic English New Testament]. Greek New Testaments have the phrase εγω ειμι (Ego Eimi), which is also used in the Septuagint in the account of Moses before the burning bush. Ego Eimi is the translation for the phrase "Ahiah Asher Ahiah"/"I AM THAT I AM" in Exodus 3:14. Clearly, this is divine speech reserved for only YHWH. That is how it was obviously understood by the translators as well as the crowd who heard Y'shua say it, evidenced by their reaction - attempting to stone Him for blasphemy.

We must all pay close attention to who it is that is speaking in a text of Scripture. In the 48th chapter of Isaiah, from verse 3 on, it is unarguably YHWH who is speaking. In fact, verse 12 in this chapter is one of the three "I am the first and the last" divine declarations found in Isaiah. Then we come to this statement four verses later;

Come near to Me, hear this: I have not spoken in secret from the beginning; from the time that it was, I was there; and now the Master יהוה has sent Me, and His Spirit. [Isaiah 48:16 ISR Version]

Now look carefully at the text of Zechariah chapter 2. Verse 8 reads;

For thus said יהוה of hosts [for the sake of esteem He sent Me to the nations which plunder you]: For He who touches you touches the apple of My eye. [Zechariah 2:8 ISR Version]

Then in verse 11, we read the following;

And I shall dwell in your midst. And you shall know that יהוה of hosts has sent Me to you. [Zechariah 2:11b ISR Version]

The three, Father, Son, and Spirit, are mentioned simultaneously in the Brit Chadashah in the gospel of Matthew.

And when Y'shua was immersed, he arose at once from the water, and heaven was opened to him, and he saw the Spirit of Elohim which was descending like a dove, and it came upon Him. Behold, and a voice from heaven that said, "This is My beloved Son in whom I am pleased.
[Matthew 3:16-17]

Go therefore, make disciples of all nations and immerse them in the Name of the Father and of the Son and of the Ruach haKodesh.
[Matthew 28:19]

All Creation Reflects the Trinity

Genesis 1:1 contains a time, space, and matter continuum that scientists did not discover until the 20th century.

In the beginning [time], God created the heavens [space] and the earth [matter].

The idea of the continuum is that these three had to have come into existence at the very same instant, simultaneously. If you create matter without time, when would you have created it? If you did not have space, where would you put it?

Time, Space, and Matter are a trinity of trinities.

Time - past, present, and future.

Space - height, width, and depth.

Matter - solid, liquid, and gas.

This 3-in-1 pattern is seen throughout all creation. Consider just these few examples:

Universe - Height, Width & Depth

The Heavens - Sun, Moon & Stars

Earth - Land, Sea & Sky

The Atom - Protons, Neutrons & Electrons

Man -Spirit, Soul & Body

Water - H_2O [2 parts hydrogen & 1 part oxygen]

Fire - Fuel, Air & Heat [none of these three can be missing to produce fire]

Family - Father, Mother, Child

The same pattern of 3 in 1 is also throughout the history of Israel and the order by which YHWH has designed for His people:

YHWH is known as the God of the 3 Patriarchs - Abraham, Isaac & Jacob
Those anointed for leadership - Kings, Prophets & Priests
Israel had three divisions - the Priests, the Levites, and the People
The Temple - Outer Court, Holy Place & the Holy of Holies

The TaNaK/Old Testament consists of 3 parts:
Torah/Law
Nevaim/Prophets
Ketuvim/Writings

The Brit Chadasha/New Testament also consists of 3 parts;
Historical Accounts of the Gospels and Acts
The Epistles
The Revelation

The Virgin

This is a very controversial verse, as many insist it has nothing to do with Y'shua of Nazareth.

Therefore, Adonai Himself will give you a sign: Behold, the virgin will conceive. When she is giving birth to a son, she will call his name Immanuel.
[Isaiah 7:14]

When reading this verse in the context of the chapter, we see that the conception and birth of this child were to be a sign to King Ahaz. Isaiah used the word עלמה Alma, which translates literally to "young woman." Those who say this prophecy is not about the virgin birth of Y'shua argue that if Isaiah meant "virgin," he would have used the Hebrew term בתולה Betulah. However, prophecy is cyclical, meaning a greater fulfillment is expected in the future. This is obviously how this verse was understood by the translators of the Septuagint [circa 250 BCE]. The seventy men who were involved in translating the Hebrew Tanak did not use the Greek equivalent for "Alma," which would have been νεανιδα Neanida. Those seventy men unanimously chose to translate "Alma" as παρθενος Parthenos, meaning "Virgin." These men understood the prophetic implication of the first messianic prophecy of Genesis 3:15, which speaks of the woman's זרעה zerah meaning "her seed." They understood that Isaiah 7:14 was expounding upon that first prophecy of a miraculous birth. Perhaps they also understood the prophetic parable that was fleshed out through the life of Sarah. She who was barren miraculously conceived to give birth to Isaac, the promised "seed" of Abraham through whom the Messiah would later be born.

There is a law of first use in Hebrew interpretation. Where a word is used for the first time, one can understand the fuller implication and ultimate meaning of that word in another passage. עלמה Alma is first found in the account of Rebekkah at the well in Genesis 24. The "Betulah" (v16) is an "Alma" [v43]. We also see עלמה Alma in the account of Moses being brought out of the Nile. His sister Miryam is watching over him from the bank of the river while he is being brought out by the daughter of Pharaoh. Amazing prophetic implications are being told here. Moses [a prophetic foreshadowing of the Messiah] is brought out of the water. Y'shua began His ministry after coming up out of the water of the Jordan River. Miryam, Moses' sister, is an "Alma" with the very name of the mother of Y'shua. Rebekkah was drawing water from the well in Genesis 24, where "Alma" is connected to "Betulah."

Adonai is my strength and my song, and He has become my salvation [yeshuah].
Then you will joyfully draw water from the springs of salvation [yeshuah].
[Isaiah 12:2-3 with Hebrew transliteration inserted]

ALMA = OLAM

There is another layer of prophetic significance to Isaiah's use of the word עלמה Alma.

The Hebrew word translated as "Everlasting" is עולם (Olam). In Aramaic, the word for "eternity" is pronounced "Alma." This is also the word for "world."

But you, Beyth Lehem Ephrathah, you who are little among the clans of
Yehudah, out of you shall come forth to Me the One to become Ruler in Yisrael.
And His comings forth are of old, from everlasting.
[Micah 5:2 ISR Version]

In the appendices of the 3rd Edition AENT, page 713, Andrew Gabriel

Roth writes;

...the fact is that "world" and "eternity" are ideas bound together in Hebraic thought. When the rabbis, for example, talk about olam haba, the world that is to come, it is also known as the eternal place. Surely, then, the use of אלמא/Alma by Isaiah, when more precise terms could have been used, hints that there is more to this prophecy than a young woman bearing a son named Immanuel! This "son" instead, is the shadow for the type of the other Son, who is born of and whose goings forth are from **eternity** [Micah 5:2], and yet he also rules the **world**, [Daniel 7:1-13]!

The "Seed" of the woman of Genesis 3:15 is the "Son" of Isaiah 7:14, born of a virgin, but His origin is from Eternity!

The various Equidistant Letter Sequences that are embedded in the verses related to this topic are shared in Chapter 35 -THE VIRGIN BIRTH CODES & Chapter 36 - THE BREAD OF LIFE CODE.

IM-ANU-EL [God with us]

...she will call His Name Immanuel
[Isaiah 7:14b]

The term "Immanuel" is formed from three Hebrew words meaning "God with us." This passage is one of the most straightforward declarations of the divine nature of the Messiah that can be found in the Tanak. Just as YHWH tangibly dwelt with His people in the Tent of Meeting, He comes to dwell with us tangibly in the person of the Messiah! One has to stretch to get around the clear pashat/literal interpretation of this declaration.

Tim Hegg writes in his article entitled The Deity of Yeshua :

"Many Jewish Sages were put to death by Rome and are venerated as being heroes of the Jewish faith. What makes Yeshua different from these in the eyes of modern Judaism, however, is that the followers of Yeshua claim He was more than a man, more than even the greatest of men. Wrapped up in the mystery of the Messiah Yeshua is the clear biblical fact that He is divine. In short, it is the fact that we believe Yeshua to be Immanuel, "God with us," that marks the ultimate dividing line between us and rabbinic Judaism. We believe Yeshua is worthy to be worshipped; rabbinic Judaism considers such worship to be idolatry."

Modern-day Rabbinic Judaism has no problem believing the

Shekinah/the Kadosh Ruach tangibly dwelt with Israel in the Tent of Meeting during the forty years of wandering. This prophecy speaks of the very same - Em Anu El, God with us. This is also the very promise that Y'shua gives to every true disciple. It is the Father, the Son, and the Spirit of whom we are told come to dwell with us in the Apostolic writings.

...he who loves me keeps my word, and my Father will love him, and **WE** *will come to him, and* **WE** *will make a dwelling with him.*
[John 14:23]

And if the Spirit of Him who raised our Master Y'shua the Mashiyach from the dead dwells in you....
[Romans 8:11a]

The Child

For to us a child is born, a son will be given to us, and the government will be upon His shoulder. His Name will be called Wonderful Counselor, Mighty God, My Father of Eternity, Prince of Peace.
[Isaiah 9:6]

An ancient rabbinical commentary on this passage states:

"The prophet said to the house of David, for unto us a child is born, to us a son is given, and he shall receive the law upon him to keep it, and his name is called from eternity, Wonderful, Counselor, Mighty God, Continuing forever, the Messiah; for peace shall be multiplied upon us in his days."
[Targum]

Punctuation of commas and periods did not exist within the original Hebrew texts. The first Hebrew title given in this list of "names" is translated as "Wonderful" ["Full of Wonder"]. The Hebrew word that means "Wonderful" is פלא (Peleh). To phonetically sound out the letter Alef [א], one must use the same three letters of Peleh in reverse. Alef is phonetically spelled אלף with the ending/sofit form of Pey [פ] on the end. The sum of the numerical value of these three Hebrew letters equals 111 [3 Ones]. The gematria of its phonetic spelling is equal to the gematria of the word "Peleh," 111. Also, the letter Alef is written with three strokes [2 Yods and 1 Hey], with a numerical value of 1, and therefore represents God, who is אחד ECHAD/ONE.

In Judges 13, we read the account of the "Messenger of YHWH" visiting the parents of Samson to announce his conception. This is what we read in verses 17 & 18;

Then Manoah asked the angel of Adonai, 'What is your name, so that when your words come to pass we may honor you?' But the angel of Adonai said to him, 'Why do you ask for my name? It is wonderful [Peleh].
[Judges 13:17-18 with Hebrew transliteration inserted]

YHWH is "Wonderful" ['Full of Wonder']. Man cannot comprehend that which is a "Wonder." If He did not remain a mystery, how would He be "Full of Wonder" and worthy of our worship?

The remaining titles only further expound upon His "Wonder."

He is the "Mighty God."

...before Me there was no God formed, neither shall there be after Me. I, even I, am YHWH; and beside Me there is no savior.
[Isaiah 43:10b -11]

He is the "Father of Eternity."

I and the Father are One
[John 10:30]

For all the fullness of Deity lives bodily in Him [Colossians 2:9]

He is the "Prince of Peace."

Peace I leave to you. I give my own peace to you.[John 14:27a]

Who was it?

Who Inspired The Prophets of Old?

Peter writes that it was "The Spirit of the Messiah."

*And they searched for the time which **the Spirit of the Mashiyach** dwelling in them did show and testify when the sufferings of the Mashiyach were to occur, and his subsequent glory.*
[1 Peter 1:11]

Peter writes that it was "The Holy Spirit."

*For at no time was it by the will of man that the prophecy came; but Set apart men of Elohim spoke as they were moved by **the Ruach haKodesh.***
[2 Peter 1:21]

Who Is Our Paraclete [Comforter, Advocate, Intercessor]?

John quotes Y'shua saying it is "The Holy Spirit."

*But I tell you the truth, it is advantageous for you that I should go; for if I do not go away, **the Comforter [παρακλητος]** will not come to you. But if I go, I will send Him to you.*
[John 16:7 Greek English Interlinear New Testament]

John writes that it is "Y'shua."

*My little children, I write these things to you so that you do not sin. And if anyone sins, we have **an Advocate [παρακλητος]** with the Father, **Jesus Christ the righteous.***
[1 John 2:1 Greek English Interlinear New Testament]

Who Raised Y'shua the Messiah From the Dead?

John quotes Y'shua saying that it would be Himself.

*Because of this, my Father loves me that I lay down my life **that I might take it up again.** No man takes it from me, but I lay it down by my own will. For I have authority to lay it down and **I have authority to take it up again,** for this Commandment I have received from my Father.*
[John 10:18]

In his first sermon, Peter preached that it was the Father.

*But **Elohim loosed the cords of Sheol and raised him** because it was not possible that he be held in Sheol.*
[Acts 2:24]

Paul writes that it was the Holy Spirit.

*And if **the Spirit of Him who raised our Master Y'shua the Mashiyach from the dead** dwells in you, he who raised our Master Y'shua the Mashiyach from the dead will also revive your dead bodies because of his Spirit that dwells in you.*
[Romans 8:11]

Who Sends The Set-Apart Spirit To Be With Us?

John quotes Y'shua saying that it is the Father.

*But the Redeemer, the Ruach haKodesh, **the One whom my Father will send** in my name, will teach you everything.*
[John 14:26]

John quotes Y'shua saying that it is Himself.

*But I speak truth to you that it is better for you that I go, for if I do not go, the Redeemer will not come to you. But if I go, **I will send Him** to you.*
[John 16:7]

Who is the Holy Spirit?

According to Paul, The Holy Spirit is the Spirit of Y'shua.

*You, however, are not in the flesh, but in the Spirit; **if the spirit of Elohim truly dwells in you. And if in anyone there is not the Spirit of Mashiyach,** he is none of his.*
[Romans 8:9]

The Holy Spirit was sent to the disciples to lead and guide them. Right?

But Luke writes that it was the Spirit of Y'shua?

*When they came into the region of Mysia, they were disposed to go from there into Bithynia, but **the Spirit of Yeshua did not permit them.***
[Acts 16:7]

Who Comes To Dwell In Us?

John quotes Y'shua saying that it is the Father and Himself.

*Y'shua answered and said to him, "He who loves me keeps my word, and my Father will love him, and **we will come to him, and we will make a dwelling with him** [John 14:23]*

Paul writes that it is the Holy Spirit.

*And if **the Spirit** of Him who raised our Master Y'shua the Mashiyach from*

*the dead **dwells in you**....*
[Romans 8:11a]

46

"Yeshua is God" Verses

In the beginning was the Miltha. And the Miltha was with Elohim. And Elohim was the Miltha
[John 1:1]

Miltha has no direct English equivalent. It can mean WORD, MANIFESTATION, INSTANCE, or SUBSTANCE, among other things. In this context, it may be best left untranslated. [footnote by Andrew Gabriel Roth in the AENT]

And Tooma answered and said to him, "My Master and my Elohim!"
[John 20:28]

...and from among whom Mashiyach appeared in the flesh, who is Elohim over all; to whom be praises and benediction, forever and ever, Amen.
[Romans 9:5]

looking for the blessed hope and the manifestation of the glory of the great Elohim and our Life-giver, Y'shua the Mashiyach
[Titus 2:13]

But of the Son, He said: Your throne. O Elohim, is forever and ever, a righteous scepter is the scepter of Your Kingdom.
[Hebrews 1:8]

In Hebrews 1:8-9, Paul quotes Psalm 45:6-7, in which King David prophesies about the Messiah.

And we know that the Son of Elohim has come and has given us knowledge that we might know the True One; and that we might be in the True One, in His Son Y'shua the Mashiyach. He is the true Elohim, and life eternal."
[1 John 5:20]

but sanctify Master YHWH [MARYAH] the Mashiyach in your hearts
[1 Peter 3:15]

Andrew Gabriel Roth translates מריא MARYAH as "Master YHWH" because MARYAH is the Aramaic equivalent of the Hebrew יהוה YHWH. This is covered in the next chapter.

Maryah

מריא MARYAH is the Aramaic equivalent to the Hebrew יהוה YHWH. MARYAH is the Name found in the Aramaic Tanak wherever YHWH was written by the original authors. In the Tanak, the Sacred Name was written down a total of 6,957 times by the authors who wrote the original scrolls. It was later replaced in 134 places by the "Sopherim" scribes with "Adonai," "Elohim," or some other circumlocution.

Throughout the Aramaic translation of the Tanak/Old Testament, as well as in the Aramaic Brit Chadashah/New Testament, מריא MARYAH is never applied to humans, as that would be as blasphemous as applying the Hebrew יהוה YHWH to humans. Nevertheless, MARYAH is used in reference to Y'shua on numerous occasions throughout the original Aramaic New Testament. Greek lacks an equivalent for this Sacred Name; therefore, the divine essence of these verses was lost to us through translation. The following are English translations directly from the original Aramaic. Andrew Gabriel Roth uses "Master YHWH" for the translation of the Sacred Name מריא MARYAH in the AENT.

For born to you all today is the Savior that is Master YHWH the Mashiyach...

[Luke 2:11]

These are the words of an angel from heaven, making this one of the most powerful texts in the New Testament for the divinity of Y'shua.

When John the Baptist gave his answer as to who he was, he quoted a prophecy in Isaiah.

I am the voice of the crying in the wilderness, "Make straight the way of Master YHWH", as Yesha'yahu the prophet said.
[John 1:23]

Shimon said to them, "Repent and be immersed in the name of Master YHWH Y'shua for the forgiveness of sins, that you may receive the gift of the Ruach haKodesh."
[Acts 2:38]

And of them also prophesied Enoch, who was the seventh from Adam, when he said: 'Behold, Master YHWH comes with myriads of His Set Apart believers."
[Jude 1:14]

He, therefore, who eats of the bread of Master YHWH and drinks of His cup and is not worthy of it, is guilty of the blood of Master YHWH and of His body.
[1 Corinthians 11:27]

I therefore explain to you that there is no man that speaks by the Spirit of Elohim, who says that Y'shua is accursed: neither can a man say that Master YHWH is Y'shua, except by the Ruach haKodesh.
[1 Corinthians 12:3]

This Scripture in Corinthians shows that, regardless of the textual evidence, the knowledge that YHWH is Y'shua can only come by revelation of the Ruach haKodesh. This verse, therefore, serves as a sort of litmus test of who is truly His.

The first man was of dust from the earth; the second man was Master YHWH from heaven.
[1 Corinthians 15:47]

And that every tongue should confess that Master YHWH is Y'shua Mashiyach to the glory of Elohim His Father.
[Philippians 2:11]

The Lamb with 7 Horns & 7 Eyes

And I looked, and in the midst of the elders stood a lamb, as if slain; and it had seven horns and seven eyes which are the seven spirits of Elohim that are sent into all the earth. [Revelation 5:6]

In the Revelation given to the Apostle John, he sees a vision of a lamb that was slain, and it has seven horns and seven eyes. Similar imagery is described by the prophet Zechariah, who speaks of a stone with seven eyes.

See the stone which I have put before Yehoshua: on one stone are seven eyes.
[Zechariah 3:9a ISR Version]

The biblical implications of "The Stone" were covered earlier in Chapter 12.

STONE - אבן

The first two letters, Aleph and Bet, spell AV, meaning FATHER. The middle and last letters spell the word BAYN, meaning SON.

The Son and the Father are indivisibly One! The Stone in Zechariah's vision shared the same characteristic of seven eyes, which John saw in the Lamb.

First, we consider the meaning of the number 7. This is the number of perfection, fullness, completeness.

A horn is a symbol of strength. To say that the lamb had seven horns is to say that its strength was perfect/complete. The lamb that John saw was all-powerful. The word for this is OMNIPOTENT, which is a characteristic unique to YHWH alone.

An eye is a symbol of knowledge. To say that the lamb had seven eyes is the same as saying its knowledge was boundless. The lamb that John saw was all-knowing. The word for this is OMNISCIENT, which is again, a characteristic unique to YHWH alone.

Later in the book of Revelation, John describes the lamb as having been slain from the foundation of the world [see Revelation 13:8], once again telling us, as prophecy has time and time again, that the Messiah has no origin. He is eternal. He shares the attributes of a deity that no created being can claim. He is all-powerful and all-knowing. He is YHWH!

Part 2

The Hidden Codes of Divinity

Introduction

Back in the early '90's of the last century, professors of mathematics at Harvard, Yale, and the Hebrew University discovered what they called a "phenomenon" in the Bible. They ran the Hebrew manuscripts of scripture through a computer process and found hidden messages embedded at equal skip distances relevant to the face text. These Equidistant Letter Sequences [ELS's], also known as Bible Codes, were determined to occur far beyond the probability of mere chance. According to mathematician Jeffrey Satinover, "...The odds of it occurring merely by chance are less than 1 in 50 quadrillion."

When codes have the same skip distance, an equal number ties the two together in an astounding way. Quite often, the skip distance itself equals the gematria of names and phrases relevant to the face text and the embedded code.

Numerous times, the four-letter Aramaic/Hebrew name ישוע Y'shua is found embedded in passages considered messianic prophecies. Others who contend that those same prophecies are not messianic and/or have nothing to do with Y'shua of Nazareth face a challenging dilemma: the improbability of astronomical odds. Quite often, the name ישוע Y'shua appears alongside משיח Mashiach in the same verse or in close proximity, as relevant to the prophecy.

It would be comical if it were not so sad that some people will plant their flag with an unequivocal declaration stating this information is false in the face of painstaking scholarly examination that has proven otherwise. Keep in mind that mathematicians have determined a ratio of less than 1 in 50 quadrillion against the probability that the Equidistant Letter Sequences exist by mere chance. Therefore, since God alone is responsible for these occurrences, He must have put them there for our benefit. Sir Isaac Newton theorized that such hidden messages could be found at equal skip distances in the Scriptures, but in his time, the means of finding them simply were not available. Only now, in our computer age, has this phenomenon come to light. We are the people of the latter days of which the prophet Daniel said, "Knowledge would increase" [Daniel 12:4].

The Hebrew Alef-bet [Sefardi Pronunciation]

Gematria- Letters- Phonetics- Meaning

1 - א - alef - first, origin, strength, thousand, YHWH

2 - ב - bet, vet - house, creation, witness, friendship, covenant

3 - ג - gimmel - bridge, ladder, the heavens, fullness

4 - ד - dalet - door, physical realm, lifting up, elevation, poor man

5 - ה - hey - Spirit, wind, breath, grace, window, Torah, revelation, YHWH

6 - ו - vav - nail, tent peg, man, imperfection

7 - ז - za'yin - perfection, time, sword, weapon

8 - ח - chet - newness, eternity, life, fence

9 - ט - tet - hidden, goodness, humanity

10 - י - yod - hand, work, YHWH

20 - כ ך - kaf, chaf - palm, blessing, redemption

30 - ל - lamed - shepherd's staff, to teach, to learn

40 - מ ם - mem - water, nations, chaos

50 - נ ן - nun - life, faithfulness, Heir to the Throne

60 - ס - sa'mek - support, eternity

70 - ע - ayin - eye, light, nations

80 - פ ף - pey, fey - mouth, word, present

90 - צ ץ - tzadai - righteous, hook, to hunt for truth

100 - ק - qof - behind, surround

200 - ר - resh - head, chief, prince, redemption

300 - שׁ - shin, sin - teeth, destruction, El Shaddai
 400 - ת - tav - cross, sign, covenant, last

Hebrew is written from right to left.

NUMBERS DON'T LIE

Every number has an assigned meaning. Reduction to a single number is achieved by adding the values of the individual digits of any given gematria.

1 א represents God who is ONE, unity, and the origin of all things.

2 ב represents friendship, witness, covenant, redemption

3 ג represents the heavens (that which is of heaven) and is the first number of fullness/completion. (three patriarchs, three parts in one Temple, three-dimensional universe)

4 ד represents the door, creation, physicality, and the earth (four matriarchs, four winds, four directions, aka "four corners of the earth." Eden was the place in time that gave access to the presence. It had four rivers. After four millennial days, the event of the Cross took place - the doorway in time that gives all mankind, past, present & future, access to the presence of God.

5 ה is Torah, Grace, and Holy Spirit revelation; that which comes from the breath of God

6 ו is man and imperfection

7 ז is perfection, completion, and fullness of time

8 ח is newness and eternity and represents the eternal One who makes all things new.

The journey through 7 [the completion of our time] leads us into the realm of 8 [eternity]! 8 represents that which is beyond time & space. This is why the Shekinah came to dwell in the camp on the 8th day.

8 = Alef's hidden gematria, since Alef consists of 3 hidden letters, [2 yods & 1 vav, which is 10+10+6] that equal 26 [2+6=8].

8 = דת/DAT, the word for "religion" in Hebrew has a gematria of 404 [dalet = 4, tav = 400]. The sum of these three digits reduces to 8.

8 = יהוה YHWH [yod=10, hey=5, vav=6, hey=5]. The sum of these numbers is 26, whose digits reduce to 8.

8 = מריא MARYAH, the Aramaic equivalent to the Hebrew tetragrammaton, YHWH . [mem=40, resh=200, yod=10, Alef=1]. The gematria of MARYAH equals 251, and these digits reduce to 8.

 8 = ישוע Y'SHUA which has a gematria of 386; [yod=10, shin=300, vav=6, ayin=70]. 3+8+6=17, which reduces to 8.

8 = אב+בן+רוח AV+BEN+RUACH [FATHER, SON & SPIRIT]. [alef=1,bayt=2,bayt=2,nun=50,resh=200,vav=6,chet=8. The sum of these numbers equals 269. These three digits reduce to 17, which further reduces to the single number 8.

8 = אבן EHVEN, the Hebrew word for STONE. [alef = 1, bayt = 2, nun =50]. 53 is the gematria of EHVEN. 53 reduces to 8.

9 ט [which is 3x3] is the number of concealment/hiddenness. The Spirit of God (like wind) is unseen, yet nine gifts and nine fruits of the Spirit are evidence of Her hidden presence.

All numbers added to 9, or multiples of 9, will reduce to that other number.

רוח Ruach has a feminine ending. Mankind is made in the image of God. It takes more than one to reflect God's image. The man/husband is a physical reflection of the Father. The woman/wife is a physical reflection of the Ruach. Giving glory to her husband, a wife takes the name of her husband -a sign of his authority upon her. She is hidden in the home, and her presence/essence is evident in the home she makes and in the children she raises. She gives glory to her husband, not to herself, just as the Ruach gives glory to the Father. She is the hidden one under his name/ authority and covered when seen by others outside her intimate family. She is the 9, leaving only the other number.

Hidden in Plain Sight

For those who deny the divinity of Y'shua, I find that their argument begins from New Testament passages. This is a faulty approach to such an argument. Every identifying mark of the legitimate Messiah, whoever He is and whenever He is to arrive, is given to us in the Old Testament. If the Messiah is to be "God in the flesh," then surely prophecies would tell us so. In other words, He either is, or He is not, regardless of one's theological sensitivities, and prophecy would surely give us this most important point of identification.

The face text of just a few Messianic prophecies gives us the following:
- THE MESSIAH HAS NO BEGINNING

    …..his going forth is from days of eternity [Micah 5:2]

- A SPECIAL MESSENGER PRECEDES THE COMING OF YHWH

The voice of him that cries in the wilderness, Prepare ye the way of YHWH…
[Isaiah 40:3]

- THE MESSIAH IS THE CO-EQUAL OF YHWH

Awake, O sword against my Shepherd, and against the man that is my
companion. [Zechariah 13:7]

"Companion" is Strong's # 5997 עמית amiyth, and denotes equality in partnership.

- YHWH SENDS YHWH

…from the time that it was, there AM I: and now YHWH Elohim, and His Spirit, have sent ME. [Isaiah 48:16]

For thus says YHWH of hosts; After the glory has He sent ME unto the nations…[Zechariah 2:8]

- ISRAEL HAS ONLY ONE KING

…behold your King comes to you: He is just and having salvation; lowly and riding upon an ass, and upon a colt, the foal of an ass. [Zechariah 9:9]

And YHWH said to Samuel, "Hearken to the voice of the people in all that they say to you; for they have not rejected you, but they have rejected ME, that I should not reign over them." [1 Samuel 8:7]

- OUR SAVIOR IS YHWH AND YHWH ONLY

I, even I am YHWH, and beside ME there is no savior. [Isaiah 43:11]

- YHWH HIMSELF IS TO BE PIERCED

And I will pour upon the house of David, and upon the inhabitants of Jerusalem, the spirit of grace and of supplications: and they shall look upon ME whom they have pierced… [Zechariah 12:10]

Code of Genesis 1:1

In the beginning God created the heavens and the earth.
[Genesis 1:1 CJB]

Hidden within the very first word of the Bible, we find the beginning of all messianic prophecy, the nature of the Messiah, the Gospel message, and the plan of salvation. בראשית B'raysheet, "In the beginning," is only the surface meaning of these six letters. Dividing them into various words, this is what we learn:

בר אשית "Bar Aysheet "Son Revealed/Manifest/Enthroned

Aysheet has three meanings, and so, in the very first word of the Bible, at the very beginning, we are told that the Son will be "Revealed" throughout Scripture. We are also being told that He will "Manifest" Himself to the world and that He will be "Enthroned" as our King!

ברית אש "Brit Aysh "Covenant of Fire

The first word of Scripture tells us that the covenant God makes with man is a "Covenant of Fire."

Our God is a consuming fire [Hebrews 12:29]

בית ראש "Bayit Raysh "House of the King

In this first word of Scripture, we are told that all creation is the House of the King, the Messiah.

Hebrew originated as a picture language. Applying the full implications of what each letter represents, along with the messages we have previously discovered, we have an astounding message that sums up the entire redemption story in the Bible's first word.

ב = House: (all physicality, the universe)
ר = Man: (the greatest man of men, the King of all kings, the Messiah)
א = an Ox: (God and the limitless Strength and Ability of God)
ש =Teeth: (that which Consumes and utterly Destroys)
י = Hand: (a closed hand representing Work)
ת = Cross: (a Sign, Covenant)

"In the House of the King, the Son Revealed will Manifest with the limitless Strength of God to Destroy the Work [of Satan] and establish a Covenant of Fire at the Cross."

The fact that the Paleo form of tav [ת] is a Cross should not escape our attention.

This first code further confirms the hidden message in the first word of the Bible. From the Yod [י] in the first word, בראשית B'raysheet, counting 521 letters seven times spells ישוע יכול Y'shua Yahkol, "Y'shua is able [to have power]." Here, the very skip of the letters speaks to us as well. 521 is the gematria of אשכר eshkar, "gift," and יהונתן Y'honatan, "the gift of YHWH." The digits of 521 reduce to 8, the number of new beginnings, but also the number of eternity and the eternal One. The gematria of יהוה YHWH [the Sacred Name] is 26, which also reduces to 8. יהוה appears in an eight-letter skip from the first Yod in the book of Leviticus.

The Hebrew word for "stone" is spelled אבן, containing the letters for Father [אב] and Son [בן], and has a gematria of 53, which also reduces to 8.

The stone the builders rejected has become the capstone. [Psalm 118:22]

He who rejects Me rejects the Father who sent Me. [Luke 10:16]

Adding up the total numerical values for all the letters of אב/Av, "Father," בן/Ben, "Son," and רוח/Ruach, "Spirit," this is what we find;

אב=3
בן = 52
רוח = 214

Adding these digits, the total equals 269. And these three digits reduce to 8 once again!

There is an inseparability with the Father and the Son, for they are One Spirit and the One True God revealed from the very first word. The embedded code in the first word of the Bible, with a skip distance that reduces to 8, is a hidden numerical message. The Eternal One, [the Father, the Son, and the Spirit], are united together in the work of redeeming mankind [to make all things new]. Y'shua is the "gift" of God, and He is able to save!

The "Seed" Code in Genesis

I will put animosity between you and the woman - between your seed and her
seed. He will crush your head, and you will crush his heel.
[Genesis 3:15]

"R. Tanhuma said in the name of Samuel Kohith: [She hinted at] that seed which
would arise from another source, viz, the King Messiah."
[Midrach Rabbah XXIII 5-6]

The Hebrew word in this verse that translates as "her seed" is זרעה
(Zera), which means "seed" with a feminine ending. It was understood
from ancient times as a prophecy of the Messiah's miraculous birth. In
total contrast to ancient rabbinical commentary, modern-day anti-
missionaries deny that this verse has anything to do with the Messiah
at all, let alone Y'shua of Nazareth. This verse has been called the
"protoevangelium" by Christian theologians, meaning the "first
messianic prophecy." Against odds of less than 1 in 50 quadrillion, the
name of "her seed" is embedded in this verse.

Starting with the Yod ['] in the phrase אשית ah'sheet, "I will put,"
counting every 69 letters three times from left to right spells ישוע
Y'shua.

There is another verse in Genesis 1 that shares this 69 skip distance.

So there was evening, and there was morning - a fourth day.

[Genesis 1:19]

Starting with the last Yod [י] in Genesis 1:19, counting every 69 letters six times from left to right spells עזר ישוע Y'shua ahzar, "Y'shua to help." That Yod is also in the 69th word of the passage about the 4th day of creation. Four represents physicality/creation.

What is 69? The number just short of 70, which represents perfection, but also the number that represents the fullness of the nations; "For all have sinned and fall short of the glory of God" [Romans 3:23]. Without Y'shua to help, mankind falls short of perfection - incapable of saving themselves.

The Bridegroom Codes

In Genesis 2:18-24, we read the account in which YHWH puts Adam into a deep sleep and forms a woman from his rib. This is a prophetic foreshadowing of the Bride being brought forth through the redemptive work of the Messiah. He is the Second Adam who was put in a deep sleep [His death], and through His sacrifice, people are redeemed from every tribe and nation [His Bride]. There are four codes embedded in these seven verses confirming these truths on a sod (hidden) level.

Then Adonai Elohim said, "It is not good for the man to be alone. Let Me make a well-matched helper for him."
[Genesis 2:18]

In verse 18, starting with the Ayin (ע) in אעשה, eh'ehseh, "I will make," counting every 138 letters three times from left to right spells ישוע Y'shua. 138 also happens to be the gematria of the letters that comprise the phrase בן אלהים Son of God.

So the man gave names to all of the livestock, and to the flying creatures of the sky, and to all the animals of the field; but for the man He did not find a well-matched helper for him.
[Genesis 2:20]

In verse 20, starting with the Mem [מ] in Adam's name, counting every 101 letters three times from right to left spells משיח Mashiach.

Adonai Elohim caused a deep sleep to fall on the man, and he slept; and He took
one of his ribs and closed up the flesh in its place.
[Genesis 2:21]

In verse 21, starting with the Mem [מ] in תרדמה tar'daimah, "deep
sleep," counting every 49 (7x7) letters three times from left to right
spells משיח Mashiach.

Adonai Elohim built the rib, which He had taken from the man, into a woman.
Then He brought her to the man. Then the man said, "This one, at last, is bone of
my bones. And flesh from my flesh. This one is called woman, for from man was
taken this one."
[Genesis 2:22-23]

In verse 23, starting with the first Lamed [ל], counting every 43 letters
four times from left to right spells לישוע leY'shua "to [for] Y'shua."

I will rejoice greatly in Adonai. My soul will be joyful in my God. For He has
clothed me with garments of salvation [yeshuah], He has wrapped me in a robe of
righteousness - like a bridegroom wearing a priestly turban, like a bride adorning
herself with her jewels.
[Isaiah 61:10 with Hebrew inserted]

Starting with the Chet [ח] in חתן Bridegroom, counting 25 letters
three times from left to right spells משיח Mashiach.

The Atonement Code

The third chapter of Genesis ends with three amazing ELS's that reveal God's plan to atone for man's sin in the righteousness of the Messiah. In the closing verses of the third chapter of Genesis, we read the account where God clothes Adam and Eve with the skin of an animal before banishing them from Eden. It is said that man and woman were clothed in "Light" before the fall. It is interesting to note that the spelling of "Light" and "Skin" is practically identical in Hebrew. "Light" is אור [aleph-vav-resh] and "Skin" is עור [ayin-vav-resh]. The clothes formed from the animal slain are a prophetic foreshadowing of our being clothed in the Light of the Messiah, which the embedded code also reveals.

Now Adam named his wife Eve because she was the mother of all the living.
Adonai Elohim made Adam and his wife tunics of skin, and He clothed them. Then
Adonai Elohim said, "Behold, the man has become like one of Us, knowing good
and evil. So now, in case he stretches out his hand and takes also from the Tree of
Life and eats and lives forever."
[Genesis 3:20-22]

As hard as it may be to wrap our minds around it, God's plan from before creation included man's fall in order that the drama of redemption would be played out through history. The plan of salvation was formed long before the rebellion of Lucifer and the anticipated sin of Adam and Eve, which is why Y'shua is called "the Lamb slain from the foundation of the world" [Revelation 13:8], because God had the remedy before creation.

From the last Yod ['] in verse 20, counting nine letters three times from left to right spells יהוה YHWH. Then, starting with the last Hey [ה] in verse 20, counting every nine letters five times from right to left spells יושיעה Yoshiah, which means "He will save"!

From the Ayin [ע] in the word for "Skin," counting seven letters twice from right to left gives a three-letter spelling of Y'shua [ישע]. Even the skip distance is relevant since 7 is the number of perfection. His work of redemption will perfect us into His image!

The Enoch Code

Enoch was the seventh descendant from Adam, and the biblical account tells us that "…Enoch walked with God…and he was not; for God took him" [Genesis 5:22-24]. There is an interesting pattern of seven when comparing Enoch with Y'shua. Counting back to Adam from the genealogy given in the Gospel of Luke, we find that Y'shua is the seventy-seventh from Adam (see Luke 3:23-38). Enoch walked perfectly with God and was taken up to God… a type and foreshadowing of our perfect Messiah.

However, on a side note, scripture tells us, "there is none righteous… all have sinned" [Romans 3:10 & 23], and therefore ALL are in need of the Savior. Also, we know that "it is appointed for all men once to die" [Hebrews 9:27]. Elijah, too, was taken, and many believe that these two will be the ones to come again as the two witnesses in Revelation. They will die when they are slain, lie dead for three days, be resurrected, and caught up before the eyes of everyone right before the greatest portion of judgment is poured out upon the world (see Revelation 11:3-13).

Now Enoch walked with God continually for 300 years after he fathered Methusaleh, and he fathered sons and daughters.
{Genesis 5:22}

Starting with the Chet [ח] in חנוך Chanok "Enoch," counting every 129 letters three times from right to left spells משיח Mashiach.

The Ark Codes

The ark of Noah has long been understood as a foreshadowing of God's salvation ["Messiah"]. Those who entered the ark were kept safe from the judgment poured out upon the inhabitants of the world. There are two Equidistant Letter Sequences in this portion of Scripture that confirm this prophetic foreshadowing.

Of the flying creatures according to their kind, of the livestock according to their kind, of all the crawling creatures of the ground according to their kind - two of everything will come to you to keep them alive.
[Genesis 6:20]

In Genesis 6:20, starting with the first Bet [ב], counting 13 letters four times from right to left spells במשיח B'Mashiach "in Messiah."

In the six-hundredth year of Noah's life, in the second month, on the seventeenth day of the month, on this day, all the water sources of the great deep burst open, and the windows of the sky were opened.
[Genesis 7:11]

In Genesis 7:11, starting with the second Tav [ת], counting 130 letters five times from right to left spells תושיעם toshiyam "You will save them." The Hebrew word toshiyah means "salvation by God through a man."

The Joseph Codes

The book of Genesis ends with the story of Joseph. He was hated and rejected by his brothers, sold into slavery, wrongly accused, imprisoned, then exalted as the most powerful man in the world, second only to Pharaoh himself.

"When his brothers saw that their father loved him more than all his brothers, they hated him and could not speak to him in shalom.
[Genesis 37:4]

In this verse, starting with the Alef [א] in the phrase וישנאו va'yis'nu, "and they hated," counting 27 letters five times from left to right spells אח ישוע ach Y'shua, "brother Y'shua."

"...please listen to this dream I dreamed."
[Genesis 37:6]

From the Ayin [ע] in the word שמע shema, "hear," translated as "listen" in the TLV, counting 214 letters three times from left to right, spells ישוע Y'shua. The letters adjacent to these spell תמים (tummim), which can be translated as Perfection, Integrity, Truth & Spotless.

Then his brothers went to graze their father's flock at Shechem. Israel said to Joseph, "Aren't your brothers grazing the flocks in Shechem? Come, let me send you to them." "Here I am," he said to him. Then he said to him, "Go now, and check on the welfare of your brothers and the welfare of the flocks and bring word

back to me." So he sent him from the valley of Hebron, and he went to Shechem.
[Genesis 37:12-14]

Genesis 37:12-14 gives us a prophetic foreshadowing of our heavenly Father sending His beloved Son to "check on the welfare" of His brothers [the shepherds of Israel] and "the welfare of the flocks" [the people of Israel].

Starting with the last Mem [מ] in verse 14, counting 117 letters three times from right to left spells משיח Mashiach.

Potiphar, an official of the Pharaoh, bought Joseph from the Ishmaelites who had brought him to Egypt. Joseph found favor with Potiphar, and so Potiphar appointed him as his personal servant and overseer of his household.

From the time that he made him an overseer in his house and over everything that belonged to him, Adonai blessed the Egyptian's house because of Joseph; Adonai's blessing was on everything that belonged to him, in the house and in the field.
[Genesis 39:5]

Starting with the 3rd to last yod ['] in this verse, counting 100 letters three times from left to right spells ישוע Y'shua.

Later, Potiphar's wife accused Joseph of wrongdoing, and Potiphar, still finding favor with Joseph, had him imprisoned rather than killing him.

But Adonai was with Joseph, extended kindness to him, and gave him favor in the eyes of the commander of the prison. The commander of the prison entrusted into Joseph's hand all the prisoners who were in the prison, so that everything that was done there, he was responsible for it. The commander of the prison did not concern himself with anything at all under his care, because Adonai was with him, and Adonai made whatever he did successful.
[Genesis 39:21-23]

Starting with the last Chet [ח] in verse 23, counting every 117 letters three times from right to left spells משיח Mashiach. This is incidentally the same skip distance as משיח Mashiach embedded from verse 14.

When Pharaoh had his dreams, Joseph was brought out from prison to interpret them.

Then Pharaoh said to Joseph, "Since God has made all this known to you, there is no one as discerning and wise as you. You! You will be over my house, and all my people will pay homage to you. Only in relation to the throne will I be greater than you."
[Genesis 41:39-40]

Starting with the last Yod ['] in verse 40, counting 100 letters three times from right to left spells ישוע Y'shua. This is the same skip distance as in Genesis 39:5 when Joseph was appointed and honored by Potiphar to rule over his household. Now, Joseph is appointed and honored by Pharaoh to rule over all of Egypt. 100 is associated with Gentile authority, as in the Centurion in the Gospels. He was a ruler over 100 men, and he honored Y'shua and "appointed" Y'shua, so to speak, to take charge in the spiritual and physical realms when he requested him to heal his servant simply by speaking the word!

Then, in the last chapter, we read the account where Joseph comforts his brothers. They fear for their lives after the passing of Jacob, their father. Surely, Joseph will take vengeance on them for the evil they had done to him when he was a boy.

...and his brothers also came and fell down before him and said, "Behold, we are your slaves!"
[Genesis 50:18]

Starting with the last Mem [מ] in this verse, counting every 40 letters three times from right to left spells משיח Mashiach.

Joseph then makes a profoundly prophetic statement regarding the Messiah and the nation of Israel.

Yes, you yourselves planned evil against me. God planned it for good, in order to

bring about what it is this day, to preserve the lives of many people.
[Genesis 50:20]

Israel's rejection of the Messiah would mean salvation for the whole world! At the end of the book of Genesis, the sons of Israel recognize who Joseph really is – the brother they hated and handed over to the Gentiles. So too, at the end of history, the sons of Israel are recognizing who Mashiach ben Yosef really is – the brother they hated and handed over to the Gentiles.

Codes of "The First and the Last"

In the 14th verses of the first and last chapters of Genesis, codes are originating from those verses at a matching skip distance of 172. In chapter one, the code spells "Y'shua." In chapter 50, the code spells "Mashiach." Notice the numbers. 14 is double perfection. The three digits of 172 reduce to 1, the number representing God.

Then God said, "Let lights in the expanse of the sky be for separating the day from the night. They will be for signs and for seasons and for days and years.
[Genesis 1:14]

In Genesis 1:14, starting with the ayin [ע] in the word מועדים mo'adim, "appointed times/seasons", counting 172 letters three times from left to right spells ישוע Y'shua. The mo'adim are the festivals that prophetically reveal Y'shua in His work of redemption for mankind.

After burying his father, Joseph returned to Egypt, he and his brothers and all those who went up with him to bury his father.
[Genesis 50:14]

In Genesis 50:14, starting with the first mem [מ], counting 172 letters three times from right to left spells משיח Mashiach.

בראשית B'raysheet "In the beginning" is also בר אשית Bar Aysheet "Son Revealed." The book of Genesis begins and ends with Y'shua haMashiach, The Beginning and the End, the First and the Last !

The "Yah" Codes

So Esau went to Ishmael and took Mahalath, the daughter of Ishmael, Abraham's son, Nebaioth's sister, for his wife, besides other wives.
[Genesis 28:9]

In Genesis 28:9, starting with the second Yod [י], counting every 19 letters 5 times from right to left spells ישוע יה Y'shua Yah.

We also saw there the Nephilim. [The sons of Anak are from the Nephilim.] We seemed like grasshoppers in our eyes as well as theirs!
[Numbers 13:33]

In Numbers 13:33, starting with the first Yod [י] in the phrase בעינינו b'ainai'nu "in our eyes," counting every 12 letters 5 times from left to right spells יה ישוע Yah Y'shua.

The Code of the Two Witnesses

An especially unusual Equidistant Letter Sequence occurs in Exodus 3, connecting the Messiah with Moses and Elijah. These two prophets are undoubtedly representations of the sum total of Torah and the Prophets. They were also the very ones who appeared at the transfiguration speaking with Y'shua.

In verse 7, starting with the Yod ['] in the phrase ויאמר va'yomer, "and said", counting every 120 letters six times from left to right spells ישועושי, which spells "Y'shua" twice in both directions, sharing the Ayin [ע], from left to right and right to left. Beyond the fact that Bible Codes have mathematically been determined to have an occurrence of less than 1 in 50 quadrillion, this is an ELS oddity - a very rare occurrence! In addition to this, the adjacent letters to Y'shua's name spell אליה Eliyah. The very skip distance of this code is also something to consider, as it is the number of years of the life of Moses! So putting this altogether, in the passage that reads, "And He said, 'I have surely seen the affliction of My people...'" [Exodus 3:7], the Messiah's name is embedded twice in both directions at a skip distance equaling the years of Moses' life, with adjacent letters spelling the name of the prophet Elijah.

The Psalm 22 Code

For dogs have surrounded me. A band of evildoers has closed in on me. They
pierced my hands and my feet.
[Psalm 22:16]

"The Patriarchs will one day rise again in the month of Nisan and will say to the
Messiah...You have been a laughing-stock and a derision among the peoples of the
world, and because of you they have jeered at Israel, as it is written [Psalm 22:6].
You have dwelt in darkness and in gloominess, and your eyes have not seen light,
your skin was cleaving to your bones, and your body withered like wood. Your
eyes became hallow from fasting, and your strength was dried up like a potsherd,
as it is written [Psalm 22:15, 22:16 Heb.]. All this happened because of the sins of
our children, as it is written: 'Jehovah laid on him the iniquity of us all' [Isaiah
53:6]."
[Pesiqta Rabbati, Friedman's edition, chapter 37]

PSALM 22 & GENESIS 22 CONNECTION

Then He said, "Take your son, your only son whom you love - Isaac - and go to
the land of Moriah, and offer him there as a burnt offering on one of the mountains
about which I will tell you."
[Genesis 22:2]

This event in Genesis 22 took place on Mt. Moriah, the very location of
the crucifixion. Men numbered the chapters and verses in the Bible,
but God was sovereignly at work even over that! The number 22

alludes to the final letter in the Hebrew Alef-Bet, Tav [ת]. In the pictograph forms of the letters, Tav is a Cross.

The Tav is a "sign." The Cross is a "sign." The question is "What is the Cross a sign of or for?" Some would say it is a sign of falsehood, of pagan religion, of Roman mixture and evil.

In Psalm 22:16, starting from the Ayin [ע] in the word מרעים m'ra'im "evildoers" and counting every 26 letters seven times from left to right, spells, אות כישוע ot k'Yshua, which means "A Sign for [of] Y'shua."

26 is the gematria of the Sacred Name. This Equidistant Letter Sequence embedded in Psalm 22 confirms the message from the pictograph forms of the four letters comprising the Sacred Name.

Yod [י] = Hand
Hey [ה] = Look
Vav [ו] = Nail
Hey [ה] = Look

When Y'shua stated that He was the "Alef and the Tav," He was not only telling us that He was the Beginning and the End. The Alef represents God, and the Tav, a Cross.

Y'shua is the God of the Cross. The Cross is the "Sign" for [of] Y'shua.

The Virgin Birth Code

Therefore, the Lord himself shall give you a sign; Behold, a virgin shall conceive
and bear a son, and shall call his name Immanuel.
[Isaiah 7:14]

This verse is quoted by both Matthew and Luke in their Gospel
accounts of the virgin birth of Y'shua. However, anti-missionary
rabbis are quick to argue that the Hebrew word translated "virgin" in
this verse is not the virgin exclusive term בתולה Betulah, but עלמה
Alma, meaning simply "damsel" or "young maiden." They do this in
total disregard of the fact that the Septuagint translators translated
עלמה Alma as παρθενος parthenos, the virgin exclusive term in Greek,
approximately 250 years before the Gospel writers. They also
disregard the hermeneutic law of first use, which directly connects
עלמה Alma to בתולה Betulah in Genesis 24.

And the girl was very fair of form, a virgin/בתולה [Genesis 24:16]

Behold, I stand at the well of water, and when the virgin/עלמה comes forth to
draw water...[Genesis 24:43]

Both Isaiah 7:14 and Genesis 24:16 contain amazing Equidistant Letter
Sequences relating to the virgin birth and Messiahship of Y'shua of
Nazareth.

In Isaiah 7:14, starting with the Mem [מ] in עלמה alma, counting every

17 letters three times from right to left spells משיח Mashiach. Continuing 17 letters in the opposite direction from the same mem [מ] three times spells כונ kavan, which means "sacrificial bread."

In Genesis 24:16, starting with the Ayin [ע] in the phrase העינה ha'an'ah "to the well", counting 386 letters three times from left to right spells ישוע Y'shua. 386 is also the standard gematria of ישוע Y'shua.

Letters spelling יונה Jonah are adjacent to the letters spelling Y'shua. Yonah means "dove," which Yochanan testified of seeing the Spirit in the form of when the Messiah came up out of the water.

In the next chapter, we'll cover the "Alma" & "Olam" connection in the 5th chapter of Micah and the code that is embedded in the prophecy about Bethlehem.

The Bread of Life Code

...With a staff, they have struck the Judge of Israel on the cheek. "But you, Beth-Lehem Ephrathah - least among the clans of Judah - from you will come out to Me One to be ruler in Israel, One whose goings forth are from old, from days of eternity."
[Micah 5:1b-2]

Son of Judah, Judaean! Tie your ox and tie your plow, for the King Messiah has been born!' ....He asked him: 'From where is he?' He answered: 'From the royal fort of Bethlehem in Judah
[The Jerusalem Talmud, Berachoth, fol. 5a]

The prophet Micah tells us the Messiah will be born in Bethlehem, whose origin is from eternity. Anti-missionary rabbis and other critics will argue that this portion of Scripture has nothing to do with Y'shua of Nazareth. However, the code embedded in this verse settles the argument as to who this verse is prophetically referring to.

Starting from the fourth yod ['] in Micah 5:2, counting every 49 [7x7] letters from left to right spells ישוע Y'shua. There are exactly 77 letters that comprise Micah 5:1-2 [Micah 4:14 -5:1 in the Hebrew Tanak]. 77 is the number of His genealogy. The Bread of Life is to be born in the town called "The House of Bread."

The Blood Codes

Then He said, "What have you done? The voice of your brother's blood is crying
out to Me from the ground."
[Genesis 4:10]

In Genesis chapter 4, we read the account of the innocent blood of Abel
shed by the hand of his brother, Cain. This is the beginning of a theme
that will run throughout the Scriptures - a theme that is inescapable. As
Andrew Murray stated, "There is no single scriptural idea, from Genesis
to Revelation, more constantly and more prominently kept in view, than
that expressed by the words – The Blood." Like the blood of the animal
sacrifices, the blood of Abel foreshadows the blood of the Messiah, and
this is confirmed by the ELS embedded in this account.

In Genesis 4:10, in the phrase קול דמי אחיך kol d'mai achakh, "the voice of
your brother's blood," starting with the Mem [מ] in the word for "the
blood", counting seven letters six times from left to right spells
משיח אמת Mashiach em'met, "Messiah truth."

A man or a woman who is a medium or is a soothsayer shall surely be put to
death. They shall stone them with rocks, and their blood shall be on them.
[Leviticus 20:27]

In Leviticus 20:27, a verse that ends with the phrase, "their blood shall be
upon them", starting with the first Dalet [ד], counting seven letters five
times from left to right spells דמ ישוע dam Y'shua "Y'shua's blood."

He who is the Kohen Gadol among his brothers, upon whose head the anointing oil is poured and is consecrated to put on the garments, is not to let the hair of his head hang loose or tear his clothes, nor should he go near any dead person, defiling himself, even for his father or his mother. He is not to go out of the Sanctuary or profane the Sanctuary of his God, for the crown of the anointing oil of his God is upon him. I am Adonai.
[Leviticus 21:10-12]

Leviticus 21:10-12 speaks of prohibitions for the High Priest, who is representative of our Great High Priest, the Messiah. Starting with the first Hey [ה] in verse 10, counting every three letters seven times from right to left spells הן דמ ישוע hain dam Y'shua "Behold the blood of Y'shua."

One final point to consider with these three ELS's....the skip distance of the first two is 7, the number that speaks of perfection - His sacrifice is perfect! The last has a skip distance of 3. The entire Godhead is involved in the sacrifice!

The Tabernacle Code

*Adonai spoke to Moses, saying, "Tell bnei-Yisrael to take up an offering for Me. From anyone whose heart compels him, you are to take My offering. These are the contributions which you are to receive from them: gold, silver and bronze; blue, purple and scarlet cloth; fine linen and goat hair; and ram skins dyed red, seal skins, acacia wood; oil for the light, spices for the anointing oil and for the sweet incense; onyx stones and setting stones for the ephod and for the breastplate. Have them make a Sanctuary for Me, so that **I may dwell among them**.*
[Exodus 25:1-8]

YHWH's Shekinah, His tangible Presence, dwelt with Israel in the Tent of Meeting while they wandered for forty years in the wilderness. In the same way, His Kadosh Presence dwelt in the 1st & 2nd Temples. Em-Anu-El, "God with Us," has been a reality for God's chosen remnant throughout all of history. In fact, the Tabernacle in the wilderness and the Temple in Israel are only shadows of the Messiah.

Y'shua answered and said to them, "Tear down this temple and after three days I will raise it!" The Yehudeans said to him, "For forty and six years this temple was built, and you will raise it in three days!" But he was speaking concerning the temple of his body.
[John 2:19-21]

In Exodus 25:5, starting with the Ayin [ע] in the word for skin, עור, counting 219 letters three times from left to right spells ישוע Y'shua. From the same [ע], counting 219 letters seven times in the opposite direction, right to left, spells אמת הירה ha'yorah em'met, which translates to both "teach the truth," and "the early rain truth."

The Yom Kippor Code

For the life of the flesh is in the blood: and I have given it to you upon the altar to make an atonement for your souls: for it is the blood that makes an atonement for the soul.
[Leviticus 17:11]

...because everything, according to Torah, is purified with blood: and without the shedding of blood there is no forgiveness of sin.
[Hebrews 9:22]

Leviticus 17 gives instructions on sacrifices to be made for atonement. The blood of animals had no power to save, but was only a type and shadow of the ultimate sacrifice and the blood to be shed by the eternal Son!

In Leviticus 17, starting with the first Hey [ה] in verse one, counting 77 letters from right to left, spells המקרה ישוע ha'miqreh Y'shua, "the event of Y'shua." The Hebrew word for meeting is also מקרה miqrah. We meet with God for the first time when we each personally come to the event of Y'shua, His atonement of our sins. The number of spiritual perfection is 7, but 77 is the amplification of spiritual perfection. This number is also the exact number of the Messiah's genealogy given in the Gospel of Luke. God is always speaking to us through numbers. Could it have been any other number? He is the 77th generation from Adam because He is the perfect and blameless Son of God! His sacrifice for us is perfect perfection! Also, the letters adjacent to ישוע (Y'shua) spell מורה, "Teacher of Righteousness." מורה also means "early rain." Yom Kippur comes in the month of Tishri during the season of the early rain. It is the Moadim/Appointed Time that represents the final atonement achieved through our Messiah, Y'shua!

The Seed Codes

In chapter 25, I shared the code embedded in the "protoevangelium," the first prophecy about the Messiah in Genesis 3:15. In that first prophecy, the Messiah is called the woman's "seed."

*Then Adonai said, "This is the land that I swore to Abraham, Isaac, and Jacob, saying, 'I will give it to **your seed**.'*
[Deuteronomy 34:4a]

Now the promises were spoken to Abraham and to his seed. It doesn't say, "and to seeds," as of many, but as of one, "and to your seed,' who is the Messiah.
[Galatians 3:16 TLV]

The land of Israel was promised to "the seed," which Paul points out is singular and refers to the Messiah. In the Messianic age, it is only those in Messiah who will enter into inheriting the "Promised land," the olam haba, that is "the world to come!"

In Deuteronomy 34:4, starting with the third-to-last Yod [י], counting nine letters three times from right to left spells ישוע Y'shua. And the adjacent letters spell תורה Torah.

*But thou, Israel, art my servant, Jacob whom I have chosen, **the seed** of Abraham, my friend.*
[Isaiah 41:8 KJV]

A common theme running through the prophet's writings is that Israel and the Messiah share parallel destinies. In other words, we often find references to Israel in which the greater fulfillment lies in the Messiah. Conversely, we can see Israel as a prophetic paradigm to the work of the Messiah. What happens to Israel happens to the Messiah, and what happens to the Messiah happens to Israel. Their destinies run parallel to one another.

Isaiah 41:8, once again, speaks of the seed of Abraham. As was pointed out in Paul's letter to the Galatians, "the seed" is the Messiah.

זרע zera is singular in this passage of Isaiah. The ultimate seed of Abraham is the Messiah, and this is also revealed by the code embedded in this verse.

In Isaiah 41:8, starting with the last Mem [מ], counting eight letters three times from right to left spells משיח Mashiach.

The Isaiah 53 Codes

Behold, My servant will prosper, He will be high and lifted up and greatly exalted. Just as many were appalled at You - His appearance was disfigured more than any man, His form more than the sons of men. So He will sprinkle many nations. Kings will shut their mouths because of Him, for what had not been told them they will see, and what they had not heard they will perceive." Who has believed our report? To whom is the arm of Adonai revealed? For He grew up before Him like a tender shoot, like a root out of dry ground. He had no form or majesty that we should look at Him, nor beauty that we should desire Him. He was despised and rejected by men, a man of sorrows, acquainted with grief, One from whom people hide their faces. He was despised, and we did not esteem Him.

Surely He has borne our griefs and carried our pains. Yet we esteemed Him stricken, struck by God, and afflicted. But He was pierced for our transgressions, crushed because of our iniquities. The chastisement for our shalom was upon Him, and by His stripes we are healed. We all, like sheep, have gone astray. Each of us turned to his own way. So Adonai has laid on Him the iniquity of us all. He was oppressed, and He was afflicted, yet He did not open His mouth. As a lamb led to the slaughter, like a sheep before its shearers is silent, so He did not open His mouth. Because of oppression and judgment, He was taken away. As for His generation, who considered? For He was cut off from the land of the living, for the transgression of My people - the stroke was theirs. His grave was given with the wicked, and by a rich man in His death, though He had done no violence, nor was there any deceit in His mouth. Yet it pleased Adonai to bruise Him. He caused Him to suffer. If He makes His soul a guilt offering, He will see His offspring, He will prolong His days, and the will of Adonai will succeed by His hand. As a result of the anguish of His soul, He will see it and be satisfied by His knowledge. The Righteous One, My Servant, will make many righteous, and He will bear their iniquities. Therefore, I will give Him a portion with the great, and He will divide the spoil with the mighty - because He poured out His soul to death, and was counted with transgressors. For He bore the sin of many, and interceded for the transgressors.

[Isaiah 52:13-53:12]

Isaiah wrote this around 700 BC. The following are a few ancient commentaries from Jewish rabbinical sources on the above portion of scripture:

"Behold, My servant shall prosper, he shall be exalted, etc. 'Behold, my servant shall deal prudently.' This is the King Messiah. 'He shall be exalted and extolled, and be very high.' He shall be exalted more than Abraham; for of him it is written. 'I have exalted my hand to the Lord' [Gen XIV 22]. He shall be extolled more than Moses...[Num XI 12]."

[Targum]

"...the Holy One will reveal to them Messiah, the son of David, whom Israel will desire to stone, saying, Thou speakest falsely; already is the Messiah slain, and there is none other Messiah to stand up [after him]; and so they will despise him, as it is written, 'Despised and forlorn of men;' but he will turn and hide himself from them, according to the words, 'Like one hiding his face from us.'"
[Mysteries of Rabbi Shim'on Ben Yohai Jellinek, Beth ham-Midrash, 155, part iii, p. 80]

And when Israel is sinful, the MESSIAH seeks mercy upon them, as it is written, 'By His Stripes we were healed, and HE carried the sins of many; and MADE INTERCESSION FOR THE TRANSGRESSORS.'"
[B'reshith Rabban, pp. 430, 671]

There are those who say the suffering servant spoken of in Isaiah 52:13 through 53:12 is NOT Y'shua of Nazareth, but rather the nation of Israel that suffered in the Holocaust of WWII, [a fairly late interpretation]. The codes tell us otherwise.

Starting with the second Yod ['] in יאריך ya'arik "He shall prolong," counting 20 letters 6 times from left to right spells ישוע שמי Y'shua

Shmi, "Y'shua [is] My name"!

Also in Isaiah 53, starting with the first Mem [מ] in verse 11, counting every 42 letters from left to right three times spells משיח Mashiach. The Shin [ש] in Y'shua is shared with the [ש] in Mashiach. This is an extra special occurrence for ELS's.

The Prince Code

Some of you will rebuild the ancient ruins, will raise up the age-old foundations,
will be called Repairer of the breach, Restorer of Streets for Dwelling.
[Isaiah 58:12]

How intrinsically connected are God's covenant people with Himself? The terms "His Body" and "His Bride" speak of that intrinsic connection. Here, in this verse, we read a prophecy concerning a future generation... a future to the people of Isaiah's day. This prophecy echoes another end-time prophecy from the book of Amos.

"In that day will I raise up David's fallen sukkah. I will restore its breaches, raise
up its ruins, and rebuild it as in days of old..."
[Amos 9:11]

When God's people are repairers and restorers, they are ultimately doing the work of the Messiah who comes to heal and restore all things. The Equidistant Letter Sequence embedded in this verse reveals whose will and work they are accomplishing.

Starting with the last Shin [ש], counting every 13 letters five times from right to left, spells שר ישוע Sar Y'shua, "Y'shua the Prince."

The Isaiah 61 Code

The Ruach of Adonai Elohim is on me, because Adonai has anointed me to proclaim Good News to the poor. He has sent me to bind up the brokenhearted, to proclaim liberty to the captives, and the opening of the prison to those who are bound, to proclaim the year of Adonai's favor, and the day of our God's vengeance, to comfort all who mourn.
[Isaiah 61:1-2]

In Luke 4:18-19, we read where Y'shua was given the scroll of Isaiah to read. He read chapter 61:1-2, but it is interesting to note where He stopped reading. It was halfway through verse 2. He stopped where it says, "To proclaim the year of Adonai's favor" and left off the two following phrases, "...and the day of our God's vengeance and to comfort all who mourn." He did this on purpose because it was not yet time for these events to be fulfilled; the day of vengeance of our God and the comforting of all who mourn. Had He read the rest of the verse, He would not have been able to state, "This day is this Scripture fulfilled in your ears" [Luke 4:21]. The day of vengeance and the comforting of those who mourn will be fulfilled at the Second Coming. This is just one example of how a Messianic prophecy speaks of the completed work accomplished through the Messiah, combining His roles as Moshiach ben Yosef and Moshiach ben David.

Few would argue that this is a messianic prophecy, but some would contest that the Messiah is not Y'shua of Nazareth. However, the code sovereignly embedded in this text removes all doubt as to whom this verse refers to.

From the first Yod [י] in the phrase רוה אדני יהוה Ruach Adonai YHWH, "The Spirit of the LORD," counting every nine letters three times from left to right, spells ישוע Y'shua. The count is also relevant since 9 is the number associated with the Gifts and Fruits that come by "the Spirit of the LORD."

The Savior Code

*"You are My witnesses" - it is a declaration of Adonai - "and My servant whom I have chosen, so that you may know and believe Me, and understand that I am He. Before Me no God was formed, and there will be none after Me. I, I am Adonai - and **there is no savior beside Me.**"*
[Isaiah 43:10-11]

This is a question every believer needs to ask themselves. "Who is my Savior?" According to what we read from the prophets in the Tanak, we only have One, and that is יהוה YHWH. Some, like Jehovah's Witnesses, for example, like to say that "Jesus is a god," but not YHWH. We call Y'shua our "Savior," but unless He is YHWH, we have a very problematic theology that does not align with scripture.

*"So now, do not fear, Jacob My servant," says Adonai, "nor be dismayed, Israel, for behold, **I will save you** from afar, your seed from the land of their exile. Jacob will again be quiet and at ease..."*
[Jeremiah 30:10]

So who exactly is doing the saving, according to the verse above?

In Jeremiah 30:10, starting with the Yod [י] in כי, the Hebrew word "for," counting seven letters three times from right to left, spells ישוע Y'shua.

The King Code

Rejoice greatly, daughter of Zion! Shout, daughter of Jerusalem! Behold, your king is coming to you, a righteous one bringing salvation. He is lowly, riding on a donkey - on a colt, the foal of a donkey.
[Zechariah 9:9]

I was watching in the night visions. Behold, One like a Son of Man, coming with the clouds of heaven. He approached the Ancient of Days and was brought into his presence. Dominion, glory, and sovereignty were given to Him that all peoples, nations, and languages should serve Him. His dominion is an everlasting dominion that will never pass away, and His kingdom is one that will not be destroyed.
[Daniel 7:13-14]

The following is from THE END OF HISTORY - MESSIAH CONSPIRACY by Dr Philip Moore, page 149:

The Talmud Sanhedrin points out that there would be two Comings as prophesied in Zechariah 9:9 and Daniel 7:13. What seems to reinforce this Talmudic interpretation is the interesting fact about the construction of the two Hebrew words that describe the Comings. The keyword "humble" in Zechariah 9:9 denotes the First Coming, while the word "clouds" in Daniel 7 denotes the Second Coming.

-end of excerpt-

The prophet Zechariah wrote in Hebrew. "Humble" in the text is עני Ani. The prophet Daniel wrote in Aramaic. "Clouds" in Aramaic is עַנָנֵי

Anani.

These two words are almost identical except that Ani, humble, is spelled with one Nun [נ] and Anani, clouds, is spelled with two. The Nun in the pictograph forms of the Alef-Bet is a fish and symbolizes "life." Joshua of old was called "Yehoshua son of Nun" - a prophetic allusion to Y'shua, the Son of Life! The placement of one Nun in Zechariah's prophecy and two in Daniel's are textual hints of the First and Second Comings for those who have eyes to see it.

> *Rabbi Joshua ben Levi asked: "In one place it is written, 'Behold, one like the*
> *Son of Man,' etc., and in another, 'Lowly and riding upon an ass!' If they be*
> *worthy, He [the Messiah] will come with the clouds of heaven; if not, He will*
> *come lowly and riding upon an ass."*
> *[Talmud Sanhedrin, fol. 98, col. 1]*

Zechariah 9:9, [like Micah 5:1-2], contains exactly 77 Hebrew letters. Starting with the first Yod [י] in the first word גילי gi'li, "Rejoice," counting 22 letters three times from right to left spells ישוע Y'shua. The 22 skip distance occurs again in Proverbs 30:4, [covered more in Chapter 49], a verse that references the Son of God. The number 22, as discussed in Chapters 4 and 34, is an allusion to the Cross, as well as the Alef-Bet of which the entirety of the Word of God is comprised.

The Zechariah 12 Codes

In that day Adonai will defend the inhabitants of Jerusalem so that the weakest
among them that day will be like David and the house of David will be like God,
like the Angel of Adonai before them.
[Zechariah 12:8]

Starting with the Mem [מ] in the phrase ביום ba'yom," in that day,"
counting 38 letters three times from right to left spells משיח Mashiach.

Then I will pour out on the house of David and the inhabitants of Jerusalem a
spirit of grace and supplication, when they look toward Me, whom they pierced.
They will mourn for him as one mourns for an only son and grieve bitterly for
him, as one grieves for a firstborn.
[Zechariah 12:10]

"What is the cause of this mourning? In this, Rabbi Dosa...said it was for
Messiah, the son of Joseph, who is to be slain...If the cause will be the violent
death of the Messiah, the son of Joseph, one can understand that which is written,
'And they shall look to him whom they have pierced.' "
[Talmud Succah, fol. 52, col. 1]

"Behold, he comes with the clouds; and all eyes will see him, and also they who
pierced him; and all the tribes of the earth will mourn on account of him. Yes:
Amen.
[Revelation 1:7]

In Zechariah 12:10, starting with the Chet [ח] in the phrase היחד ha'yachid, "an only son," counting 38 letters three times from left to right spells משיח Mashiach.

The Betrayal Code

*All who hate me whisper together about me. They imagine the worst about me:
"Something evil was poured into him - he will not get up again from the place
where he lies."*
[Psalm 41:8-9]

This is the shortest equidistant letter sequence known, with only a
two-letter spacing. Starting with the first Yod ['] in the phrase יחשבו
רעה yach'shvu rah'ah, "they plot evil," skipping to every other letter
three times from right to left spells ישוע Y'shua. The four letters that
were skipped spell חברה (chavrah), an association, group, family, or
assembly.

Also, starting with the second-to-last Yod ['] in verse 9, counting 14
letters six times from right to left spells ישוע חלי Y'shua chali, "Y'shua
the polished jewel."

The Resurrection Code

You went up on high. You led captivity captive. You received gifts from humanity,
even from the rebellious - so that God might dwell there. Blessed be my Lord! Day
by Day He bears our burdens - the God of our salvation! Selah
[Psalm 68:18-19]

The apostle Paul expounds on the prophecy above, telling us it refers to the Messiah's ascension from the heart of the earth.

Therefore, it is said: "He ascended on high and carried captivity away, and gave
gifts to men. Now that he ascended, what is it but that he also previously
descended deep into the heart of the earth?
[Ephesians 4:8-9]

Peter also, by the inspiration of the Holy Spirit, tells us this in his first epistle.

And he preached to those souls who were detained in Sheol [Hades]
[1 Peter 3:19]

Matthew records in his Gospel that, after the Messiah's resurrection, holy ones also rose with Him. The resurrection took place on the Jewish festival known as HaBikkurim, the Festival of Firstfruits. Together, with Messiah, they were the firstfruits from among the dead.

And the tombs were opened, and many bodies of the Set Apart believers who were asleep arose, and went out. And after his resurrection, they entered into the Set Apart city and were seen by many.
[Matthew 28:52-53]

For as it was by Adam that all men die, so also by the Mashiyach they all live: Everyone in his order; the Mashiyach was the first-fruits; afterwards, they that are the Mashiyach's, at his coming.
[1 Corinthians 15:22-23]

By His resurrection, death was conquered! When the veil was torn in the Temple, it was only a sign of the greater breakthrough that He had obtained. He has opened the way of life eternal for everyone!

In Psalm 68, starting with the first Ayin [ע] in verse 19, counting 344 letters three times from left to right spells ישוע Yshua with the adjacent letters spelling הפלש ha'phah'lash, "to break open or through."

The Son Code

Who has gone up into heaven, and come down? Who has gathered the wind in the palm of His hand? Who has wrapped the waters in a cloak? Who has established all the ends of the earth? What is His name, and what is the name of His son - if you know?
[Proverbs 30:4]

Skeptics who do not believe in the deity or Messiahship of Y'shua will deny that this passage from Proverbs has anything to do with Him. One explanation is that the "son" being referenced is simply the nation of Israel. However, this verse contains the very name of the son it speaks of, not once, but twice!

Starting with the Yod [י] in the last word for "Who," [מי] in this verse, counting 22 letters five times from right to left spells ישוע שי Y'shua shai, Y'shua the Gift. Then, at a 300-letter skip from right to left from that Ayin [ע] in Y'shua, the name Y'shua is spelled out again, but in reverse.

Y'shua is the gift of God to mankind. This precious gift does no one any good unless they turn from their sins and toward Him. We must believe to receive Y'shua the Gift!

The Daniel 9 Code

Seventy weeks are decreed concerning your people and your holy city, to put an end to transgression, to bring sin to an end, to atone for iniquity, to bring in everlasting righteousness, to seal up vision and prophecy, and to anoint the Holy of Holies. So know and understand: From the issuing of the decree to restore and to build Jerusalem until the time of Mashiach, the Prince, there shall be seven weeks and 62 weeks. It will be rebuilt, with plaza and moat, but it will be in times of distress. Then, after the 62 weeks, Mashiach will be cut off and have nothing. Then the people of a prince who is to come will destroy the city and the sanctuary. But his end will come like a flood. Until the end of the war, it is decreed that there will be destruction.
[Daniel 9:24-26]

Although this prophecy contains precise details about the time of the Messiah's appearance in history, many anti-missionary rabbis and others deny that it has anything to do with Y'shua. I have heard it said that the Angel Gabriel was giving Daniel details about King David's past. Another theory is that Gabriel was speaking of King Cyrus. The events that later transpired in history, as well as the code embedded, tell us otherwise.

There is so much contained in this prophecy. To stay on task with the subject matter of this book, I will point out just a few important points before sharing the hidden message of the code.

First, the phrase משיח נגיד (Mashiyach Nagid) in this passage translates as "Messiah cut off," meaning "killed." This prophecy states that the Messiah will "bring sin to an end," and "atone for iniquity and bring in everlasting righteousness." Then, after the Messiah is "cut off," "the people of a prince" [the Romans] "will destroy the city" [Jerusalem] "and the sanctuary" [the Temple]. From this prophecy alone, we know that if the Second Temple is no longer standing, the Messiah has already come.

The code embedded in this passage is at a 26-letter skip and originates from verse 26. 26 is the numerical value of "YHWH," reminding us twice again of who Y'shua, our Messiah, truly is. Starting from the Yod [י] in the phrase והעיר "and the city," [as it is worded in the Hebrew], counting 26 letters 3 times from left to right spells ישוע "Y'shua."

Credits

Introduction: Dr. Daniel Botkin - Gates of Eden Vol. 30 No. 5, page 11

Chapter 1: Rabbi Tzvi Nassi & Dr. Al Garza -The Great Mystery: How Can Three Be One? And Yeshua in the Ancient Hebrew, pg.13

Chapter 7: The Great Mystery: How Can Three Be One? And Yeshua in the Ancient Hebrew by Rabbi Tzvi Nassi & Dr. Al Garza ThD, PhD, pages 121 -130

Chapter 10: Benjamin Sommer - Bodies of God, pp 41-42

Chapter 16: Andrew Gabriel Roth - 3rd Edition AENT, page 713

Chapter 17: Tim Hegg - Excerpt from article entitled The Deity of Yeshua

Chapter 20: Andrew Gabriel Roth - footnote on John 1:1, 3rd Edition AENT, pg. 232

Special Thanks to Ya'acov Rambsel for his book Yeshua, the name of Jesus Revealed in the Old Testament, September 1996, Frontier Research Publishing, whose research was the basis for Section 2 of this book, THE HIDDEN CODES OF DIVINITY.

www.ingramcontent.com/pod-product-compliance
Lightning Source LLC
Chambersburg PA
CBHW041335120726
48005CB00014B/2272